BET... ____
THE STATE
AND THE
SCHOOLHOUSE

THE EDUCATIONAL INNOVATIONS SERIES

The Educational Innovations series explores a wide range of current school reform efforts. Individual volumes examine entrepreneurial efforts and unorthodox approaches, highlighting reforms that have met with success and strategies that have attracted widespread attention. The series aims to disrupt the status quo and inject new ideas into contemporary education debates.

Series edited by Frederick M. Hess

OTHER BOOKS IN THIS SERIES

BETWEEN THE STATE AND THE SCHOOLHOUSE

Understanding the Failure

of Common Core

———————

TOM LOVELESS

HARVARD EDUCATION PRESS

Cambridge, Massachusetts

Paperback ISBN 978-1-68253-590-5
Library Edition ISBN 978-1-68253-591-2

Library of Congress Cataloging-in-Publication data is on file.

Published by Harvard Education Press,
an imprint of the Harvard Education Publishing Group

Harvard Education Press
8 Story Street
Cambridge, MA 02138

Cover Design: Endpaper Studio
Cover Photo: Jemastock/Shutterstock

The typefaces used in this book are Adobe Garamond and Minion Pro.

To the memory of
Jan Talbot (1925–2007) and Sandy Cognini (1944–2002),
strong, talented women who were dear friends, amazing colleagues,
and two of the best teachers I have ever known.

CONTENTS

INTRODUCTION

The Common Core State Standards (CCSS) represent one of the most ambitious American education reforms of the past century. Developed in 2009 and released in June 2010, the standards were designed to define what students should learn in mathematics and English language arts (ELA) from kindergarten through the twelfth grade. States already had their own individual standards and assessments, but many analysts considered them weak and ineffectual. By the end of 2010, more than forty states and the District of Columbia had adopted the CCSS as official K–12 standards. Even nonadopting states wrote new standards that mirrored key elements of CCSS. Swept away were fifty diverse sets of state-crafted standards, along with their attendant assessments and accountability systems.

The standards enjoyed early political support. US Secretary of Education Arne Duncan declared that CCSS "may prove to be the single greatest thing to happen to public education in America since Brown versus Board of Education."[1] A bipartisan coalition of elites, including nearly all of the movers and shakers in education policy, promoted CCSS. But a political backlash emerged—and it, too, was bipartisan. Opponents on the right objected to the federal government's support of the standards, warned of the dangerous precedent of allowing Washington to meddle in curriculum matters, and derided CCSS as "Obamacore." Opponents on the left blasted the new assessments associated with the standards, objected to teacher evaluations tied to test scores, and organized opt-out movements that informed parents of how to exclude their kids from state testing programs.

A decade later, scant evidence exists that Common Core produced any significant benefit. One federally funded evaluation actually estimates that the standards had a negative effect on student achievement in both reading and math. Fortunately, the overall impact is quite small.

A strange aspect of Common Core is that politicians have sent mixed signals on whether it even exists. When the Every Student Succeeds Act was signed into law in 2015, US Senator Lamar Alexander declared, "The federal Common Core mandate is history."[2] And yet in 2016, Donald J. Trump ran for president promising to get rid of Common Core, characterizing it as a federal mandate.[3] In 2017, US Secretary of Education Betsy DeVos told a radio audience, "There isn't really any Common Core anymore," and she emphatically declared to a 2018 audience at the American Enterprise Institute, "Common Core is dead."[4] A year later, the governors of two states, Florida and Georgia, announced plans to end Common Core in their states, despite DeVos's pronouncements and the standards of both states having been previously rewritten to get rid of Common Core.[5]

If we conclude that CCSS had a minimal impact on student learning, perhaps the standards changed other aspects of education in a productive manner. Even if such a possibility is conceded, the policy's extraordinary costs and the ferocious debate that it engendered outstripped such meager benefits. Billions of taxpayer dollars, from both federal and state coffers, were poured into making CCSS a success. Prominent philanthropies, led by the Bill & Melinda Gates Foundation, funded a public relations campaign to fight back against political opposition. The nation's three-million-plus public school teachers were asked to retool their instruction and use new curriculum materials aligned with Common Core; large numbers of students began failing new Common Core–aligned assessments; and many parents struggled to understand the strange new homework assignments that students were bringing to the kitchen table.

Future historians will look back on this era and ask: What was Common Core? Where did it come from? What was the big Common Core debate all about? Why did the standards fail to produce the outcomes promised by advocates? Those questions lead to a final and important one: What are the lessons from the Common Core experience that can inform future education policy and research? In tackling these questions, four themes cut across chapters and emerge from the book's narrative.

IMPLEMENTATION ISN'T EASY

A phrase heard repeatedly after the Common Core State Standards were released was, "Of course, standards are only the beginning; it all depends on their implementation." Implementation of large-scale, top-down education policy transpires in a complicated system that is multilayered and loosely coupled in terms of authority and expertise. Common Core is not a federal policy, although it received crucial support from the federal government during the Obama administration, but it is national in scope, originally involving more than forty states and Washington, DC. States have their own political offices and educational bureaucracies, of course, but consider some ballpark numbers for the nodes of political and organizational authority situated below the state level: approximately 13,600 school districts (also democratically governed and administered by professional bureaucracies), 98,000 schools, and more than three million teachers, most working in their own classrooms. Navigating the vertical complexity of the K–12 educational system is daunting.[6]

Saying that standards depend on implementation is a bit like saying skydivers' enjoyment of the day depends on their parachutes opening. Fortunately for skydivers, the probability of a chute failing is infinitesimal. Not so for the odds of top-down policies encountering obstacles on the way to local sites of implementation. This was illustrated in a classic 1973 study, *Implementation*, by Jeffrey L. Pressman and Aaron Wildavsky. The study analyzed the Economic Development Administration, a jobs development program targeting urban areas. Pressman and Wildavsky studied the program's impact in Oakland, California. The program received ample funding and enjoyed bipartisan political support at federal, state, and local levels of government, along with the support of major stakeholders in the private sector. And yet it failed miserably, with a barely a hint of the program's existence three years after federal funds first reached Oakland.[7]

What happened? Pressman and Wildavsky introduce the concept of *decision points* to explain the difficulty of policies navigating multilayered systems of governance. A decision point could involve any person or agency—political or bureaucratic or even outside of government—with the power to disrupt a policy's implementation. Each layer (state, district, school, etc.) may have several decision points to clear before implementation can proceed. Consider an implementation path in which the probability of negotiating any single decision point is quite high. An early estimate of the probability of successful implementation may lead one to predict that implementation will be easy. That's probably what Common Core developers were thinking as they worked with the representatives of governors and state school chiefs in 2009: "Everyone is in agreement here; we should be able to get this done." Such reasoning overlooks that the probability of success shrinks as the number of decision points increases. For a policy with a 95 percent probability of clearing a single decision point, it takes fourteen decision points for the odds to drop below 50 percent, making failure more likely than success. Michael Q. McShane calculated seventeen decision points for Common Core, most at the state level alone, and reported that a state official took him to task for undercounting the true number.[8]

Common Core was not a jobs program with a dedicated stream of revenue fed into local budgets. In that respect, the odds of successful implementation are probably longer than one would estimate using Pressman and Wildavsky's conceptual scheme. Standards-based reform succeeds by changing what schools teach and how they teach it—by changing behaviors, not by writing checks. The policy lineage for CCSS can be traced to state efforts to regulate curriculum and instruction, which date back to the nineteenth century.

Common Core is similar to the policies promoting tracking reform that I studied in the 1990s, research that I published in a 1999 book, *The Tracking Wars*.[9] *Tracking* is the practice of grouping students into separate classes by prior achievement or differentiating subject matter by difficulty. Some eighth graders, for example, may take a general math class, while more advanced students take Algebra I. At the high school level, Advanced Placement (AP) classes are offered in most academic subjects. Middle schools in California and Massachusetts were urged by state policy to reduce the amount of tracking in favor of classes with students who were heterogeneous in ability. Tracking is highly controversial. Critics charge that separating students by ability or prior achievement inevitably creates classes segregated by race and socioeconomic background and that offering different curricula to tracked classes exacerbates existing achievement differences. Opponents of detracking often include parents of high-achieving children, who want accelerated curriculum options for their children beyond the conventional grade-level program.

I found that schools' implementation of tracking reform differed by school subject and several local conditions. Math teachers were resistant and continued offering differentiated classes—in particular, Algebra I courses to advanced eighth graders—while teachers of ELA and other subjects were more likely to embrace reform and create heterogeneously grouped classes. Organizational characteristics of schools influenced how schools responded. Middle schools are structured by varying grade levels. Schools with sixth to eighth grades were receptive to detracking, but those with seventh to eighth grades or seventh to ninth grades were resistant. The former are often staffed with elementary-trained teachers who have experience with heterogeneously grouped classrooms; the latter typically are not. Schools serving large numbers of students were more likely to continue some form of differentiation, but schools with smaller enrollments were more likely to adopt heterogeneously grouped classes. Increased school size is correlated with a wider span in student achievement.

The main lesson of the study was that schools shape state policies to fit local circumstances. Schools' demographic characteristics also predicted their response to tracking reform. Consistent with the argument that detracking serves the cause of equity, schools most likely to embrace detracking were located in urban areas and served students predominantly from low-income households. Schools located in suburban areas and serving more socioeconomically advantaged families, on the other hand, resisted the reform and were more likely to continue with tracking.

UNPREDICTABILITY

Common Core's developers were well aware that without changes in key aspects of schooling, the standards they were writing would be rendered inert. No one knows, when standards are written, released, and adopted, how that will all play out. Curriculum and instruction are particularly important because they constitute the technical core of the educational enterprise, producing the learning that takes place in classrooms. They sit at the bottom layer of the system. Writing and adopting standards takes place at the top of the system, in the domain of politicians and educational officials, often informed by experts. Authority shifts downward as standards are implemented. Curriculum and instruction are under the control of teachers, principals, and local educators. Successful implementation of standards not only depends on the willingness of implementers but also on the quality of the curriculum and instruction that local educators use to enact the standards.

The quality of curriculum and instruction varies in several ways. The publisher of a terrific K–8 math series may also publish a terrible reading series; a math program with strong second and sixth grade texts may be weak in first and fourth grades; a fifth-grade ELA text may be effective in building vocabulary and offer engaging writing prompts, but spotty on grammar, spelling, and the fundamentals of writing. In addition, teachers do not teach in a vacuum. They respond to their students by modifying curriculum or altering teaching when necessary. They seek out supplementary materials when those provided to them are not appropriate. Sometimes teachers make adjustments on the fly. Lucky is the veteran teacher who has not experienced the dreaded day when an instructional unit that has always worked well falls flat with a particular cohort of students.

The odds of successfully implementing standards would be vastly improved if perfection in everything that matters downstream were guaranteed. Of course, it's not. There are good teachers and bad teachers and those in between. There is good curriculum and bad curriculum and a lot in between—and the same is true for assessments and accountability systems. Excellence in any of these domains is not easy to accomplish. It may even be difficult to define. Each has its own set of experts, research methodologies, and scholarly literatures. Experts in accountability systems are often economists and political scientists who know very little about pedagogy. Moreover, experts in the curriculum and instruction of particular school subjects rarely venture across disciplinary borders. Scholars of early literacy instruction are not expected to know the research on teaching secondary mathematics or science. An expert on teaching Shakespeare or Faulkner to AP English students probably won't be appointed to a blue-ribbon commission evaluating elementary math textbooks.

POLITICS AND IDEOLOGY

The two subjects that Common Core tackles, mathematics and English language arts, have long histories of ideological debates between educational progressives and traditionalists. In the 1980s and 1990s, the disputes came to be known as the *reading wars* and the *math wars*. The terms for the debates and the protagonists are clumsy, but they refer to a real phenomenon. Some version of this ideological struggle has been going on since the dawn of the twentieth century, and, as we will first encounter in chapter 1 and revisit in later chapters, the politics of progressive-traditionalist conflict play a role in Common Core's story. Let's save more on that point for the book's narrative. The idea here is to alert readers that navigating multiple decision points also places implementation in constant political jeopardy. Defeated parties are never vanquished; they can always resurface and fight again in another forum. Common Core supporters won a number of victories in state adoptions that were later modified or overturned. In addition, social media serves as a platform for organizing opposition. The careful crafting and precise wording of math standards dimmed in importance to the ridicule that a few notorious homework problems generated, fairly or unfairly, after going viral. Ideology infuses topics beyond curriculum and pedagogy, too, as illustrated by the opt-out protests, a grassroots movement philosophically opposed to standardized testing that stood against Common Core assessments.

REFORM POLICIES ARE INCREMENTAL

American education reform is frequently characterized as a series of waves that rise and fall or as a pendulum swinging back and forth between contending social values.[10] Policies emphasizing excellence and equity are good examples. The 1950s policies coming after Russia's launch of the Sputnik satellite focused on enhancing America's standing in the world. The role of advanced mathematics and science in national security received special attention. Those policies were followed by the

1960s reforms of the Great Society and civil rights era, with heightened efforts to improve the education of impoverished, Black, and Hispanic children, long neglected by US schools.

The reform efforts inspired by *A Nation at Risk* in 1983 have a slightly different dynamic. Each successive decade produced policies designed to raise student achievement, but they also tried to fix a perceived weakness of previous policy efforts. Immediately after *A Nation at Risk*, states instituted minimum competency tests and raised course content and graduation requirements. But many analysts felt these policies focused too much on basic skills. The 1990s featured professional organizations writing national standards and states adopting curriculum standards that included higher-level skills and content, backed by periodic assessments and school accountability systems. Critics considered the assessments too infrequent and the accountability systems more bark than bite. No Child Left Behind was passed and prevailed over most of the 2000s. It mandated annual testing in reading and math for the third through eighth grades and an accountability regime that ratcheted up sanctions on schools falling short. States were allowed to write their own content standards and to decide the level of student performance demonstrating proficiency on student assessments, provided that all students met that level by 2014. By 2009, the goal of 100 percent student proficiency was criticized as a cruel pipedream; a majority of schools in the country were rated as failing and in danger of incurring penalties. Moreover, the states' standards and assessments were seen as uneven in quality. The time was ripe for a set of shared, grade-by-grade standards in math and ELA. Common Core was born.

ORGANIZATION OF THE BOOK

This book is organized in eight chapters. The first three chapters are histories. The fourth and fifth chapters are on the content of the standards, early implementation, and politics. The sixth and seventh chapters review the existing empirical evidence on Common Core's effects. Finally, the eighth chapter concludes the book.

Chapter 1, The Roots of State-Led Reform, describes the development of state powers over schools, the ongoing ideological struggle between educational progressives and traditionalists, and the emergence of scholars who brought scientific expertise to the study of curriculum and instruction. Classroom activities that had once been the sole domain of local educators were now influenced by forces beyond the schoolhouse walls.

Chapter 2, Rising Expectations, Competing Ideas, begins with the reforms prompted by *A Nation at Risk*, details the rise of systemic, standards-based reform in the 1980s and 1990s, and ends with the passage of No Child Left Behind.

Chapter 3, Developing the Common Core State Standards, traces the decline of No Child Left Behind and the rise of Common Core.

Chapter 4, Content of the Core, reviews the content of the Common Core standards in English language arts and mathematics, pointing out strengths and weaknesses, including identifying standards that promised to be easy and difficult to implement. Foreshadowing the next chapter, it also highlights aspects of the standards destined to provoke political controversy.

Chapter 5, Resistance and Rebellion, describes how Common Core's early popularity waned as critics raised objections, especially on social media, and a well-organized political opposition arose. Opponents forged a left-right coalition, with those on the left objecting to Common Core's testing regime and those on the right concerned about the federal government's involvement.

Chapter 6, Effects on Student Achievement, reviews research on Common Core's impact on student achievement, including National Assessment of Educational Progress (NAEP) test score gaps associated with racial and ethnic groups and between high and low achievers.

Chapter 7, Effects on Curriculum and Instruction, reviews research on how curriculum and instruction changed in response to Common Core.

Chapter 8, Whatever Happened to Common Core?, summarizes the book and offers lessons for future policy and research.

A PERSONAL NOTE

When the first draft of the Common Core State Standards was released, I was a senior fellow studying education policy at the Brookings Institution in Washington, DC. A group of us in the policy field would regularly meet for a beer or two on Friday nights. The standards were the big policy topic in Washington at the time. I was repeatedly asked what I thought of them. I would shrug my shoulders and answer something like, "I don't know; we'll see how they turn out." Standards never look the same in schools as they appear on paper. When pressed on whether I had read the standards, I said that I had; when asked to evaluate them strictly in comparison to previous standards on compositional qualities, I replied, "They're better than most, but not perfect. I'd give them a B or B- as a grade."

I also would sometimes reply that I thought standards were overrated as an instrument of school reform. Many of my friends were true believers in Common Core, and they would be irked by this observation. They were ready to debate the finer points of the Common Core, perhaps even to concede that a few of the standards were a bit faulty, but they were not going to consider, not for a single second, that the whole project may be a waste of time. To them, the choice was between Common Core and an alternative set of standards, with each state's current standards as the default. I was a skeptic, not an opponent.

My earliest encounters with standards undoubtedly influenced my skepticism. When I completed my year-and-a-half teacher training program at the end of 1978, I had taken, as an elementary grade teacher candidate, instructional methods courses in math, reading, language arts, science, and history/social studies. California adopted state frameworks in each of these subjects, and they were presented as the backbone of the curriculum that we trainees would be teaching once we entered the classroom. The practice lessons we developed and textbooks we poured over were organized around the frameworks. At the time, California had textbook adoption at the state level. Publishers were given the frameworks so they could produce textbooks reflecting the state's wishes, and the books were field-tested in hundreds of classrooms for a full year (we called the process *pilot testing* and the prospective books *pilots*). The state would gather information from the field tests and adopt a list of approved texts in grades K–8 (high school texts were adopted by districts). Districts would pick books from the approved list.

The state also had an annual test, the California Assessment Program (CAP), given in selected grades with matrix sampling, a new technique used also by NAEP. Unlike NAEP, scores from CAP were produced for each school, and it was a momentous day each year when the scores were published in local newspapers. The scores were also scrutinized every three years by a team of educators from outside the district, part of the Program Quality Review. This was California's version of the United Kingdom's inspectorate system, with schools visited periodically, classrooms observed, and a report issued that described strengths and weaknesses at the school and suggestions for ways to improve.

I taught until June 1988, when I left the classroom to enter a PhD program at the University of Chicago. Oddly enough, it was not my own personal experiences as a teacher that shaped my thinking on standards. The jobs I took isolated me from their reach. My first year of teaching was in a self-contained special education class—twelve kids and two aides. All of the students were at least two years below grade level, and their Individualized Education Programs (IEPs) governed the curriculum presented to each student. I then taught sixth grade for eight years in a Rapid Learner Program, in which all of the kids were on the other end of the achievement spectrum, about two years above grade level. As rapid learner teachers, my colleagues and I had unusual autonomy to select curriculum materials. Most of the books I used were pitched at approximately the eighth-grade level, many of them old and out of print so that my students wouldn't encounter them again in later grades.

What left a lasting impact on my view of standards was observing the politics of standards, especially as it evolved at the state level, from my perch in the classroom. Bill Honig had come into office as state superintendent of public instruction in 1983, full of ideas and enthusiasm. And, although we didn't know it then because the term wasn't in use, Honig was indeed a standards-based reformer. He assiduously watched over the rewriting of the state's frameworks in all academic subjects, tightened up linkages between curricular standards and existing assessment and accountability systems, and drove school reform toward the vision of a complete liberal arts education for all students.

But there were immediate troubles. First of all, the standards themselves were dominated by progressive pedagogy.[11] The 1985 Math Standards urged the de-emphasis of arithmetic and computation skills in the elementary grades. The 1992 version of the math standards went further in embracing constructivist pedagogy. The content of the mathematics curriculum, the central topic of previous frameworks, did not appear until page 75. The 1987 language arts framework never used the term *whole language*, but its student-centered focus was interpreted as endorsing alternatives to code-based approaches to reading instruction. Decades later, Honig looked back on what happened to the state's reading policy and declared, "The framework was hijacked by the whole language movement."[12]

As a teacher, I enjoyed reading education history and was especially interested in the philosophical clashes between education progressives and traditionalists. In most of the debates regarding content, I leaned toward the traditionalist side, although I considered my pedagogy to be a hybrid of progressive and traditional practice. I arranged student desks in clusters of seven or eight, for example, and assigned a lot of group projects. One favorite was a stock market unit in which, after several lessons on equities and how markets function, the clusters acted as mini mutual funds in a class competition. One of the parents bought a large coffee dispenser for the room, the kids brought mugs and instant hot chocolate from home, a class set of each morning's edition of the *Sacramento Bee* was unpacked and distributed, and the first half hour or so of each day began with students' wrangling over whether to buy IBM or Ford, plotting their portfolios' progress on large sheets of graph paper hung on the walls. When I talk to former students today—they are in their forties and fifties—and tell them that I am considered an education traditionalist, they chuckle. They don't remember much that was traditional about our classroom.

At Chicago, my intellectual interests drew me to education policy. Over the course of my career as an analyst, the policies on which I have focused most intently are those featuring heated political battles, including standards. Controversial policies always involve fundamental questions about education. Common Core fits the bill. The content of curriculum, how teachers teach, who should decide expectations for kids and how high should expectations be—these are key questions that Common Core touches upon. Like my study of tracking reform in the 1990s, the question of implementation also comes into play. Once governments have decided on a policy decision, how does it become enacted in schools? Exploring that question compels an examination of the schools system's organizational structure and the flow of policy downward from policymakers to practitioners.

Common Core has many ardent supporters and many dedicated opponents. I hope both find this book to be a fair account. I also hope readers get as much joy out of reading the book as I did researching and writing it.

THE ROOTS OF
STATE-LED REFORM

As an instrument of school reform, the Common Core State Standards attempt to influence curriculum and instruction, with *curriculum* defined as what teachers teach—in other words, the content that students are intended to learn—and *instruction* defined as how teachers teach it. The CCSS represent the latest manifestation of more than a hundred years of such reform efforts. This chapter examines a past reform era, beginning in the late nineteenth century and extending into the early decades of the twentieth century, when state governmental efforts to regulate curriculum and instruction spread throughout the United States.

Let's set the stage by looking abroad. The United States was not the only country in which schools, traditionally under the control of local officials, were increasingly seen as requiring the intervention of central authorities.

PAYMENT BY RESULTS

In the middle of the nineteenth century, suspicions grew among Great Britain's leaders that the nation's schools were doing a poor job of educating the young—in particular, the children of workers and the poor. Great Britain's school system consisted, in effect, of three separate systems serving upper-, middle-, and lower-class families. A commission was appointed in 1858, headed by the Duke of Newcastle, to investigate the issue, resulting in a six-volume report published in 1861. Known as *The Newcastle Report on Popular Education*, the report pointed to several decades of success in expanding access to education. In 1803, enrollment had totaled approximately five hundred thousand. By 1858, more than 2.5 million students were enrolled in the schools of England and Wales, out of 2.6 million children of school-going age, with the increase mostly due to higher enrollment in schools serving working-class families.[1]

The commission focused on elementary schools serving the lower classes. The report does not linger over accomplishments. Its historical importance lay in its condemnation of British education and the later policies that the critique inspired. A census conducted for the study found that only 20 percent of enrolled students were twelve years old or older. Adolescents ended their studies to join the labor force. Nearly a third of students attended school less than one hundred days per year, and those who regularly attended, the report found, "do not, in fact, receive the education they require." It was this last charge that drew the attention of policy makers. The commission declared:

> First, that all the children who attend the elementary schools of the country should be induced to attend with sufficient regularity to enable them, within a reasonable period, to obtain mastery over the indispensable elements of knowledge, reading, writing, and the primary rules of arithmetic; secondly, that all the schools in the country at winch the children of the poor attend should be qualified and induced to put this amount of instruction within the reach of their pupils; and thirdly, that this should be done in such a way as not to lower the general standard of elementary instruction to this its lowest level of usefulness.[2]

Defining educational quality by what and how much students learn— and linking that definition to the pursuit of social equity, albeit a Victorian version of it—ushered in an era of British school accountability with elements familiar to twenty-first century readers. The power of central authorities to govern schools greatly expanded. Under the Revised Code of 1862, schools would receive government funds based on attendance, the quality of school facilities, and the results from annual examinations of pupils in reading, writing, and arithmetic, conducted by outside inspectors and administered in both oral and written form. The last criterion became known as Payment by Results (PBR), a test-based accountability regime that lasted more than thirty years.

The policy was controversial from the start. Robert Lowe, vice-president of the Education Department and author of the plan's principal regulations, argued that existing school accountability was "vague and indefinite," with enforceable performance standards for educators practically nonexistent. The government promised to install a rational system of finance, with clear incentives for educators to teach students the skills and knowledge needed for adult life. Lowe also urged adoption of the plan "so that the public may know exactly what consideration they get for their money," reflecting the increasingly dominant view in London that the government's expenditures on social programs should be judged on how efficiently they produced valuable outcomes.[3]

Prior to PBR, teachers were semipublic servants, paid by mail directly from the national government. Soon after the plan's implementation, opponents of the new remuneration system charged that teachers were demoralized by the constraints placed on classroom work. They argued that the curriculum had been narrowed to only the three tested subjects, and, because the standards on which examinations were based called mostly for recitation of memorized material, instruction had been reduced to drill and rote learning.[4] Pupils were examined on a hierarchy of six standards in each subject, only proceeding to the higher standard if the lower standard had been successfully met.[5]

Thirty years is a long time for any education policy to survive, let alone one with persistent opposition. But the system looked quite different at the end of its tenure than it had at the beginning, as key provisions were incrementally chipped away. A formal review, known as *The Cross Report of 1888*, detailed several unintended consequences of the incentive system, including teachers and headmasters cheating on exams and diverting results-based revenues to schools' general budgets to offset decreases in other sources of funding. By the end of the nineteenth century, the army of inspectors and examinations that had enforced the system was viewed as cumbersome and too expensive to operate nationwide. The system faded away and is generally considered a failure today.[6]

COMMITTEE OF TEN

The first US high school was founded in Boston in 1821. Seventy years later, high schools were elite institutions; the education of nine out of ten American youth ended, at the latest, upon completing eighth grade.[7] Public schools providing an education up through eighth grade were known, not insignificantly, as *common schools*. They were open to all. High schools were politically vulnerable, especially during hard economic times, as opponents labeled them a frivolous expense, teaching future workers Latin or Greek instead of useful, employable skills. The public high school's institutional competitor was the private academy, which, after collecting tuition well out of the reach of working families, prepared children for professional careers or college. As William J. Reese notes in *The Origins of the American High School*, these threats to high schools' existence inspired, in a sense, a curriculum with a split personality. High schools had to teach knowledge and skills that were practical enough to earn taxpayers' support while also competing with the academies' offerings of high-status knowledge.[8]

As the nineteenth century progressed, high schools proliferated across the land. Public school officials urged their communities to see high schools as distinctly middle class because, as Paul Peterson explains, "such institutions lent prestige to the entire public-education enterprise . . . public schools could clearly establish themselves as something other than charity institutions expected only to instruct the children of the poor."[9] As William J. Reese reports, in 1904, US Commissioner of Education William T. Harris offered an estimate of the growth of high schools. Harris counted 11 high schools in 1850, 44 in 1860, 160 in 1870, 800 in 1880, and 2,526 in 1890. High schools were spreading rapidly, but precise numbers are difficult to determine because of no generally accepted definition of what a high school *was*. Harris only counted schools with a two- to four-year curriculum consisting of graded, advanced subject matter. In big-city high schools, admission tests to gain entry and annual exams to attain promotion to the next grade were taken for granted. Rural areas were less formal, and a high school could simply be the upstairs room where students received instruction after completing the elementary grades. Reese notes that Maine alone claimed 143 high schools in 1874, an impossible feat under Harris's criteria.[10]

Harris's long career in public education started as a teacher in St. Louis, where he later served as a school principal and superintendent (1868–1880). Benjamin Harrison appointed Harris US commissioner of education (1889–1906), a position he held under four presidents. In

1892, Harris joined a historic effort to bring order to the high school curriculum and its relationship to college. The Committee of Ten was created by the National Education Association and headed by Charles W. Eliot, president of Harvard University. In addition to Harris and Eliot, it included four other college presidents, three high school principals, and a college professor.[11] Eliot and Harris were two of the most prominent education reformers of the era, having published dozens of articles in both academic and popular journals.

Harris's lofty position in government—and the body of scholarship he produced as a philosopher, particularly his studies of Hegel—belies the nuts-and-bolts perspective he brought to the Committee of Ten. Harris's fame as the St. Louis superintendent highlighted his organizational acumen. Schools needed a rational structure, and that was especially true in a booming frontier city such as St. Louis. As historian Lawrence Cremin puts it:

> Harris's answer was the graded-school, organized by years and quarter years of work, with pupils moving through on the basis of frequent and regular examinations. For the system to function at all, planning and order were needed; and Harris's superb sense of detail never rested as he sought constantly to improve economy and efficiency. He devoted himself to attendance reports, to textbooks, to the collection of school statistics, to the standardization of pedagogical terminology, to the lighting, heating, and ventilation of school buildings, to teacher salary schedules, and to the continuing supervision of instruction. And his Hegelian love of institutions sustained him through every step of the way, for in the completely evolved system would lie the finest educational expression of the new urban civilization.[12]

The Committee of Ten report recommended four possible courses of study for high school students, all featuring academic subjects and differing mainly in terms of classical or modern languages. The four courses would prepare students not only for college, but also for life, the committee argued, and the report insisted that colleges grant admission to students successfully completing any of them. The committee also rejected the practice of curriculum differentiation based on a student's perceived destination. All students would receive essentially the same liberal education.

The Committee of Ten did not confine its recommendations to high school. Content experts issued conference reports that included recommendations on curriculum and instruction in each academic subject down to the early primary years.[13] The conference report on natural history, for example, urged that the study of plants should commence, without books, no later than the second grade; that pupils should study "the plant as a whole, not merely a part, as seeds, leaves, flowers"; and that "study should not be restricted to flowering plants, as trees and weeds, but should be extended as well to flowerless plants, such as ferns, horsetails, mushrooms and toadstools, mosses, lichens, fungi, and fresh and salt-water algae." Teachers of young children were urged to have them draw plants, explaining, "A drawing gives better ideas of form and of relations of parts than can be given by verbal description. It will be found that often the simplest and quickest way for pupils to get clear, sharp ideas about the objects they are studying is to have them draw the objects."[14]

PROGRESSIVE EDUCATION

The Committee of Ten report drew immediate fire from educators who believed that traditional academic subjects already received too much attention in the school curriculum. They were followers of what became known as the *progressive education movement*. Three ideological tenets infused progressive curricular reform: that school subjects should be useful, of practical, real-world value; should be child-centered, meaning that the topics studied should be accommodative to student interests; and should be active, involving projects that liberated pupils from books and deskwork. Whole-school designs implementing these ideals sprang up in many private schools, such as the Lincoln School, a lab school associated with Teachers College, Columbia University in New York City, but a few public systems also gained renown for system-wide reform. Schools in Bronxville (New York), Winnetka (Illinois), and Denver became famous nationally, and elements of their curricular innovations were adopted by other districts.[15]

Progressives would not rely on schools to change themselves. Lawrence Cremin begins the third of his three-volume history of American education, *The Transformation of the School: Progressivism in American Education, 1876–1957*, by telling the story of Joseph Mayer Rice, a New York City pediatrician turned journalist. Beginning in 1892, Rice wrote a series of *Forum* articles, eventually collected into a volume published in 1912, *Scientific Management in Education*. The book culminated two decades of activism. Rice had traveled to several cities in 1892 (the year the Committee of Ten met) and documented dreary, recitation-bound classrooms, dominated by instruction that he dubbed "mechanical." Two decades later, Rice's confidence that change would happen had dissipated. Herbert M. Kliebard explains, "Rice's genuine dismay and disgust of what was going on in American schools in the 1890s had evolved into a grim determination that teachers and administrators must be *made* to do the right thing. Supervision, for example, would take the form of seeing to it that the achievement of students reached a clearly defined standard."[16]

Rice believed in testing students to measure what they had learned. For his 1890s tour, in addition to producing vivid descriptions of classroom life, he had devised a number of assessments that he personally administered. Those results documented startling differences in student performance from city to city. An eight-item test of arithmetic, for example, revealed that the highest-performing city's pupils answered an average of more than seven items correctly, whereas pupils in the worst-performing city averaged less than one correct answer. In spelling, he discovered that test scores at schools devoting more than forty minutes of instruction per day to the subject scored no higher than those with ten to fifteen minutes of daily instruction. The chapter presenting the spelling data is titled "The Futility of the Spelling Grind."[17]

Rice's analysis of the data posed a question that emphasized efficiency: What could teachers be expected to accomplish in a reasonable amount of time? Here's how he explained it: "The element of time is the saving clause. If we were to demand results alone, we should be in danger of going back to the methods employed in the 'old-fashioned, mechanical schools.' But this cannot occur when we limit the time in which the prescribed results must be secured; for if more than a reasonable time is absorbed in accomplishing the demanded results, the school is below the standard."[18] Testing in the pursuit of efficiency became a

hallmark of educational progressivism. Rice described how his test results could drive the evaluations of entire school systems, explaining
how each subject (then called *branches*) would be assessed:

> In spelling, words are dictated to the children in columns and sentences.
> In arithmetic, a set of questions covering such work as is undertaken in
> all schools is given. In language, a story is read to the children, and
> the pupils reproduce it in their own words. The penmanship may form
> a part of the test in language. The papers will show the legibility and
> neatness of the handwriting, etc. By subjecting the pupils of the schools
> of different cities to the same test in any one branch to which the plan
> is applicable, we can, without doubt, get at the comparative standing of
> different cities in that branch, and substitute facts for opinions in regard
> to whether or not the teachers of those cities have been successful in the
> teaching of that branch. If in arithmetic, for instance, the questions are
> so selected, grade for grade, that no exception is taken to them by the
> teachers of any city, and the results show that the pupils in city A can
> do the examples without any difficulty while those of city B can scarcely
> do them at all, then the facts prove that the children in A are a great
> deal stronger in arithmetic than those in B, and that there is probably
> something radically wrong with the arithmetic in B.[19]

Testing grew in sophistication. By 1918, over one hundred standardized achievement tests were in use to measure student learning.[20]
But one test, the high school admission test, had faded away as public
demand for high school attendance made such selectivity unthinkable.
Philadelphia's Central High School ended entrance examinations in
1900.[21] In 1912, Pittsburgh was among the last major school systems
to abandon an admissions test.[22] High schools were increasingly in demand, and the shift from admission based on performance (exams) to
credentials (certificates of grammar school completion) threw open the
schoolhouse doors. Enrollments boomed. From 1890 to 1930, the number of students in public high schools basically doubled every decade.
As David F. Labaree notes, "Shifting to admission by grammar-school
certificate ended the exclusivity of the high school by providing a
mechanism for gaining admission that was accessible to large numbers
of students."[23]

CARDINAL PRINCIPLES
OF SECONDARY EDUCATION

Education historians often present the Cardinal Principles of Secondary Education, published in 1918, as the antithesis of the Committee of Ten. The Cardinal Principles were authored by the Commission on the Reorganization of Secondary Education (CRSE), cosponsored by the National Education Association and the US Bureau of Education. As David L. Angus and Jeffrey E. Mirel point out: "Indeed the CRSE seemed to utterly repudiate the position of the Committee of Ten regarding the importance of subject matter as a basis for high school curriculum development. Instead of Core Subjects or subject areas, the CRSE identified seven 'objectives' for secondary education: 1. Health. 2. Command of fundamental processes. 3. Worthy home membership. 4. Vocation. 5. Citizenship. 6. Worthy use of leisure. 7. Ethical character."[24]

The commission endorsed curriculum differentiation based on student interests, aptitudes, and aspirations, believing that a broadening of the types of courses offered—meaning more nonacademic courses—would lead to greater numbers of students staying in high school. The seven objectives of the Cardinal Principals are so vague and encompass so many aspects of human existence that studying almost anything could be justified as meeting their call. Herbert M. Kliebard observes that the Cardinal Principles "gave secondary schools license to expand the curriculum almost indefinitely."[25]

In his 1914 study of state control and centralization of education, August William Weber describes recent state statutes that required school districts to teach particular subjects, along with tighter state guidance on the courses comprising each subject. Although the high school curriculum remained, in Weber's estimation, largely influenced by colleges, "increasing state control of the elementary curriculum is thus plainly recognizable, and constitutes one of the significant centralizing tendencies taking place in the educational administration."[26] Instruction was rarely the target of state policy except for one key exception: mandates that all teaching be conducted in English. In 1914, three states included the mandate in their constitutions, and fourteen others had passed laws to such effect; Colorado and Louisiana allowed instruction in a foreign language under certain conditions.[27] World War I fueled American nationalism and anti-immigrant sentiments. By 1923, the number of states mandating instruction exclusively in English rose to thirty-five. Curriculum dictates regarding national heritage and civic duty also spread. Forty-three of the nation's forty-five states required the study of US history, twenty-nine required studying the history of the state, and thirty-nine required the study of citizenship.[28]

As progressive education blossomed, a broad movement to reform the school curriculum swept over education, bringing scientific principles to the field of curriculum studies. In his dissertation on the California textbook adoption process, James Allan Lufkin notes that terms such as *vocabulary burden, calibration of difficulties,* and *scientific selection of textbooks* began cropping up in educational journals, along with checklists, rating scales, score cards, and time studies as means of evaluating texts.[29]

W. W. Charters and John Franklin Bobbitt were two of the most important pioneers of curriculum studies. Both believed in judging education by its social efficiency—that is, by the school's success at training students for adulthood. They believed curriculum could be constructed scientifically through *activity study,* a form of task analysis that consisted of observing the activities of adults, breaking them down into separate tasks and skills, codifying the skills as measurable learning objectives, and then backward mapping those objectives onto the school curriculum:

> Bobbitt's objectives offered a fascinating mix of straightforward academic expectations ("the ability to get the essential thought of books or articles quickly with a minimum amount of reading," p. 46), the bizarre ("ability to make a hat frame," p. 18), and the pedestrian ("ability to select proper utensils for preparation of food," p. 19). Bobbitt also crafted objectives that signaled attention to the kinds of critical-thinking skills that many reformers assumed were neglected in the past, such as the "ability to collect, organize, and interpret facts involved, and to arrive at sound conclusions" (p. 34).[30]

As Herbert Kliebard argues, it took the nineteenth-century reform of *grading* (also called *classifying*) students—subdividing a school by placing students in a particular grade, originally irrespective of age and based on what they knew—to serve as the organizational precursor to learning objectives arrayed hierarchically across grade levels.[31] In Klieb-ard's words, "Grading, in other words, created the structural framework for a curriculum in the modern sense to emerge. At a minimum, grad-ing implied that learning expectations exist, above and beyond text-books, for groups of students to master at a more or less uniform rate."

Bobbitt and Charters took this a step further by beginning at the end, a desired outcome, and then describing the discrete learning objec-tives that would produce the desired result. Linking the proper content to each grade took expertise. As age-grading took hold, and students were expected to move through the grades with an age cohort, select-ing appropriate content became even more complex. The science of curriculum development became the province of experts, with its own arcane terminology and protocols. Curriculum would no longer be left to teachers, school principals, or elected school boards.

CALIFORNIA CURRICULUM STUDY

In 1924, California Superintendent of Public Instruction Will. C. Wood appointed William Chandler Bagley to lead a study of the state's curric-ulum and make recommendations for reform. Bagley was a skeptic of educational progressivism.[32] He was a professor at Teachers College, the intellectual center of the movement, where his colleagues included John Dewey, an esteemed educator and philosopher; and William Heard Kilpatrick, author of *The Project Method* and a leading theorist on cur-riculum and instruction. Bagley thought progressivism's emphasis on utilitarian topics, student interests, and active learning often led to the neglect of traditional academic subjects. Bagley considered himself an *essentialist*, one who believes that the main job of schooling is to pass on the intellectual achievements of humanity from one generation to the next.[33]

Bagley appointed George C. Kyte, a fellow essentialist and professor at Washington University, as resident director of the study. Research be-gan in 1924, and the final report was issued in 1926. The introduction to the report provides a summary of findings and recommendations. Bagley and Kyte make the case for a common curriculum taught to all children: "It would be most fortunate if there could be agreement upon a *core curriculum* in which the grade placement of crucial topics in the fundamental subjects would be fairly uniform throughout the State. The marked mobility of the population and other factors affecting the progress of pupils in California clearly point to the need for such an agreement. In fact, evidence was obtained in a number of the studies which strongly suggests the need for a nation-wide agreement in this matter."[34] Illustrating what a *core curriculum* entailed, Bagley and Kyte described a small number of key subjects and fundamental topics anchored to particular grades. The report chastised "curriculum congestion," caused primarily by legislative mandates, noting that before a reform law was passed in 1925, California's elementary teachers were required to teach thirty-two subjects. Most of the subjects had been championed by special interest groups and progressive devotees of prioritizing practical skills over academic content. Legislation passed in 1925 eliminated some subjects and consolidated others, reducing the number required by the state to twelve and permitting a maximum of three additions by local districts.

Figure 1.1 presents a screenshot of key topics that Bagley and Kyte recommended in reading and math.

The California Curriculum Study inspired 1927 legislation that would have a lasting impact on the state's schools: the establishment of the California State Curriculum Commission. The commission was empowered to recommend textbooks for adoption by the State Board of Education, to establish minimum standards for courses of study that all public elementary and high schools in the state must follow, and to monitor curriculum issues that may arise in the state's public schools.[35] In practice, the commission soon established a precedent that by recommending minimum standards for courses of study, it would not prescribe a particular curriculum, a concession to local educators in the perpetual tug of war between state and district authorities over what schools taught.

The reforms enhanced the influence of experts on textbook adoptions. Along with more than twenty other states, predominantly in the South and West, California featured state textbook adoption for grades K–8, enshrined by a constitutional amendment passed in 1884 and lasting throughout most of the twentieth century.[36] Unlike most of the other adoption states, California contracted with publishers to purchase or lease textbook content and printed its own versions of texts at a state

FIGURE 1.1.   *Reading and math topics, California Curriculum Study, 1926*

SUMMARY AND GENERAL RECOMMENDATIONS   31

1. Suggested Core in Reading and Literature

GRADE I. Activities and experiences directly preparing pupils for learning to read; oral and silent reading in which the basic vocabulary shall be the list determined in the Horn studies of young children's vocabularies; mechanical aids to reading utilized.

GRADE II. Oral and silent reading with less stress upon oral reading than in the first grade; a wider use of a wealth of reading matrials; continued use of mechanical aids to reading.

GRADE III. Oral and silent reading with increased stress upon silent reading; mechanical aids to reading used with much less intensity and frequency; use of a classroom library.

GRADE IV. Marked stress upon silent reading. some oral reading; mechanical aids used only with exceptional cases or in exceptional reading situations; increased attention to library reading and to literature; use of the children's library.

GRADE V. Very largely silent reading; considerable guidance in the study of literature; fixing elementary library reading habits.

GRADE VI. Silent reading; oral reading at infrequent intervals; the study of literature given large amount of the reading time.

GRADES VII and VIII. Reading literature as phases of the junior high school course in English.

2. Suggested Core in Arithmetic

GRADE I. Incidental number work; counting.

GRADE II. Very largely informal arithmetic experiences; in the latter half of the year some definite attention to the reading and writing of numbers.

GRADE III. Addition and subtraction.

GRADE IV. Multiplication, division, and introduction to simple fractions.

GRADE V. Fractions, decimals, use of denominate numbers, and aliquot parts.

GRADE VI. Percentage, measurements, simple accounts, and ratio; increased attention to problem solving.

GRADE VII. Owning, buying, selling, lending, and borrowing; interest, measurements, and introduction of equations.

GRADE VIII. Arithmetic of private life and business life.

The subject matter of the seventh and eighth grades, largely providing experiences in which the fundamentals of arithmetic are being used, can be modified to meet the needs of various groups of pupils. Such modifications may affect the program in such a way that during the last year such studies as algebra, commercial arithmetic, and elementary bookkeeping may be undertaken.

printing press in Sacramento.[37] By creating a new agency that would screen and recommend textbooks to the state board, the 1927 legislation expanded the powers of the state bureaucracy and opened a new avenue for education experts to influence policy.

If Bagley and Kyte thought they had struck a blow for essentialism, they would soon be disappointed. Education progressives had a firm foothold throughout the state—and especially in the California State Department of Education. Writing in *California Historical Quarterly*, Irving J. Hendrick describes Helen Heffernan, chief of the Bureau of Elementary Education from 1925 to 1965, as "an energetic Dewey disciple," adding that "probably more than anyone else, she was responsible for delivering the progressive message to every city and hamlet in the state." Hendrick also emphasizes the significance of long bureaucratic tenure: "State boards and superintendents came and went, but the Department of Education's Helen Heffernan remained to lead the state-directed program of progressive education."[38]

The Curriculum Commission published *Teachers Guide to Child Development* in 1932, directed at kindergarten and primary teachers, and followed it up with a version targeting teachers in intermediate grades in 1936. The guides de-emphasized academic subjects in favor of activity learning, which often involved groups of children engaged in construction projects. Historian Diane Ravitch describes children building a pet park in Los Angeles, a Raggedy Ann house in Stockton, and a playhouse in San Diego. High schools were not immune to the antiacademic fervor of the movement.[39] Hendrick summarizes the results of a 1936 survey of high school principals: three-fifths proudly reported that their schools were deemphasizing grammar; courses on practical problems of adult life were on the rise, such as teaching boys and girls about their future (gender-based) roles in a well-functioning family; and nearly half claimed to be making courses more dependent on pupil activity.

DISTRICT REFORM: PROGRESSIVISM IN DENVER

As the California survey indicates, state reforms did not produce monolithic change. Even school districts possessed limited power to enforce instructional dictates. In *How Teachers Taught*, Larry Cuban analyzes courses of study, teachers' diaries and other records, photographs of students and teachers in classrooms, journalistic accounts, and student recollections of their classroom experiences.[40] He documents the slow, incremental changes that occurred in classroom teaching from 1880 to 1990, despite several waves of reform that had washed over schools. In districts that became famous in the 1920s for promoting progressive curricula "relevant to life situations," change often occurred more on paper than in the content taught to students. In one humorous example, course catalogs in Denver tried to portray Latin courses as having real-world, practical value.

Cuban's description of how Denver's school reform unfolded in the 1920s illustrates other aspects of how change transpires in education. When Jesse Newlon arrived as Denver's school superintendent in 1920, he found a receptive audience for changing curriculum and instruction. Newlon devised a dual, bottom-up, top-down structure for curriculum creation, with a constant cycle of revision to keep the curriculum up to date. The district established thirty-seven teacher-led committees, composed of classroom teachers, school administrators, and district staff. Between 1920 and 1930, the committees revised thirty-five courses of study from elementary grades through high school. Cuban estimates that between 30 and 40 percent of instructional staff participated on at least one committee's work.

The democratic process of creation was followed by authoritarian implementation. Principals were commanded to make sure the new courses were taught. Cuban quotes a message from the district office: "In the installation of new courses the principal must be the leader in his school . . . The principal must conduct a program of study and discussion of the new course before it is ready to go into the classrooms of his school . . . It is assumed that if a principal takes an unusually long time to get a new course into classroom use he will be able to give good reasons for such delay."[41]

What difference did the Denver reforms make in classrooms? The district sought to shift instruction from teacher-centered to student-centered practices. Cuban categorized instruction as student- or teacher-centered using five criteria: the arrangement of the classroom (desks and chairs arranged in rows facing the teacher's desk and the blackboard counted as teacher-centered); student involvement in group work (whole class instruction counted as teacher-centered); classroom talk (teachers leading discussions or lessons devoted to teachers' explanations or questions counted as teacher-centered); student choice of tasks and projects (teachers deciding on classroom work counted as teacher-centered); and freedom of movement (a preponderance of seat work counted as teacher-centered).

Cuban found evidence that although a substantial percentage of teachers adopted some of the reforms, those that did created a hybrid instructional approach that mixed the old with the new. Most teachers continued to employ teacher-centered practices, especially in high schools. Elementary school teachers appeared more receptive to the progressive reforms. In summing up, Cuban estimates progressive practices were embraced by no more than one-third of teachers in the lower grades and one-fifth of high school teachers. And the fact that even teachers sympathetic to progressive ideals combined new and old approaches led him to conclude that instructional reforms are fundamentally changed when they come in contact with the daily realities of classrooms.

CONCLUSION

Historians often present *The Committee of Ten* and *Cardinal Principles* as historical bookends, grand documents signaling who was up and who was down in the ideological war between defenders of traditional academic subjects and progressive education. That is true, but not the focus here. These philosophical battles motivated educators to join *movements*, which, regardless of the particular ideological bent, inevitably sought to encode beliefs in policy and practice. No matter who was temporarily winning the philosophical contest, the struggle generated an ever-increasing number of instruments for removing authority over the curriculum from educators working in schools and placing it in the hands of experts and public officials outside the school.

School systems were booming. K–12 public school enrollment grew from 12.7 million pupils in 1890 to 25.7 million in 1930. But the major spurt in K–8 enrollment had already occurred in the nineteenth century; it is in grades 9 to 12 that growth was eye-popping. As noted earlier, public high schools basically doubled enrollment every decade from 1890 to 1930, going from 203,000 to 4.4 million students.[42]

During the formation and expansion of public school systems in the 1800s, states and districts waged a seesaw battle over controlling various aspects of schooling.[43] That battle continued in the twentieth century. States had constitutional authority over school systems, but they were not equipped to run schools; they delegated administration to school districts. Thomas B. Timar points out that in 1900 the payroll of state departments of education totaled 177 employees, counting chief state school officers. Five states had only state chiefs and no other staff. Employees of state departments in 1930 numbered nearly 1,800. The bureaucracies were growing rapidly but still quite small. They could pass regulatory edicts or make recommendations concerning curriculum and instruction, but they possessed no practical means of enforcing them.[44] No American state was in the position to attempt the type of centralized control of schools presented at the beginning of this chapter, the United Kingdom's Payment by Results program.

By 1930, education was viewed as an important state function, enshrined in all state constitutions, and the architecture was in place for future attempts at influencing curriculum and instruction. Age-graded schools allowed for the delineation of school subjects in logical progressions and the approximate matching of a curriculum to a student; textbooks and standardized tests provided tools for centralization and standardization of learning across communities. And as the elements of schooling grew in sophistication, experts—a lot of them—were needed to train future teachers and administrators, to develop new curricula and assessments appropriate for a modern age, to study how teachers instructed students and recommend better ways of teaching, and to staff the state departments and district offices or to consult with incumbents of those offices.

These elements were firmly established in 1930 and, more than fifty years later, would be marshaled by school reformers who wanted to raise expectations for America's school children.

2

RISING EXPECTATIONS, COMPETING IDEAS

L ike the end of the nineteenth century, the end of the twentieth century was ripe with education reform. In 1983, a federal commission
appointed by US Secretary of Education Terrel H. Bell released *A Nation
at Risk*, a document that joined the Committee of Ten report and the
Cardinal Principles as one of most important education documents in
American history. The report famously deplored the state of America's
schools by declaring: "If an unfriendly foreign power had attempted to
impose on America the mediocre educational performance that exists
today, we might well have viewed it as an act of war."[1] *A Nation at Risk*
insisted on higher expectations throughout the school system, recommending that high school graduation requirements include four years
of English; three years of mathematics, science, and social studies; two
years of foreign language for college-bound students; and a half year of
computer science.

The time of *A Nation at Risk* was one of economic insecurity and
heightened international competition. The United States suffered the
worst recession since the Great Depression from July 1981 to November
1982 as the Federal Reserve dramatically raised interest rates to combat inflation. The unemployment rate hit 11 percent.[2] The report named
Japan, South Korea, and Germany as economic powers that had taken
the lead on producing goods that the United States once dominated. "If
only to keep and improve on the slim competitive edge we still retain
in world markets, we must dedicate ourselves to the reform of our educational system for the benefit of all—old and young alike, affluent and

poor, majority and minority. Learning is the indispensable investment required for success in the 'information age' we are entering."[3]

Japan not only scored near the top of countries participating in international math and science tests, but its exports—especially electronics and cars—were dominating American consumer purchases. Citing declining scores on the Scholastic Aptitude Test (SAT), critics charged that the nation's level of student achievement had fallen, failing to appreciate either that the decline was at least partially due to the changing composition of students taking the SAT or that the test is an inappropriate gauge of national learning. Nevertheless, the impression stuck that something needed to be done about American schools.[4]

THE STATES RESPOND

In *Left Back*, a sweeping history of American school reform in the twentieth century, Diane Ravitch points out that "*A Nation at Risk* was a call to action."[5] States responded by raising high school graduation requirements and implementing exit exams. Studies of course taking in the 1980s reveal sharp increases in students completing academic courses. Ted Bartell and Julie Noble found increases from 1982 to 1988 in the number of students completing the courses recommended by *A Nation at Risk*, ranging from an 11 percentage point gain in completing four years of English to a 20 percentage point gain in completing two or more years of foreign language.[6]

Unfortunately, evidence that the effect on course taking produced more learning is less than convincing. Brian Jacob summarizes the research on the impact of these policies:

> What is the evidence on the effect of requiring high school students to take more rigorous courses? The results to date are mixed. There is some evidence that increased course taking boosts student performance and high school completion (Achieve, Inc., 2013). But there is countervailing evidence that higher course requirements are associated with decreases in high school completion (DeCicca & Lillard, 2001). Moreover, there is substantial evidence that high school exit exams, a closely related policy, increase drop-out rates, particularly among low-income

students (Dee & Jacob, 2007; Jacob, 2001; Jenkins, Kulick, & Warren, 2006; Papay, Murnane, & Willett, 2010), and little evidence that they improve student achievement (Dee & Jacob, 2007; Grodsky, Kalogrides, & Warren, 2009).[7]

State legislators assumed an activist role in passing laws to improve schools, and state education officials shifted accountability from procedural checklists, designed to monitor inputs, to assessments and other measures designed to measure outputs. As Joseph Murphy observes, the result was a "major shift in the locus of quality control from school districts and colleges of education to the state."[8] States also targeted curriculum, and several state leaders, including Bill Clinton of Arkansas, James Hunt of North Carolina, Richard Riley of South Carolina, and Roy Romer of Colorado, used the moment to propose ambitious reforms.

President George H. W. Bush called an education summit in 1989, bringing together the nation's governors in Charlottesville, Virginia, to establish education goals. Six goals were set for the year 2000, with one explicitly addressing academic excellence: "American students will leave grades four, eight, and twelve having demonstrated competency in challenging subject matter including English, mathematics, science, history, and geography." Curriculum frameworks, spelling out what students should know and be able to do in key subjects, were the tools states favored to pursue this goal. English language arts (ELA) and mathematics received special attention, and by 1992, thirty-five states had adopted frameworks in ELA and thirty-eight states in math. Backed by standardized assessments, state curriculum frameworks promoted a shift in power over the content of school subject matter from local schools and districts to the state.[9]

The federal government also got involved in setting standards. Although barred by federal law from recommending particular curricula, the Bush administration funded standards-writing projects by major professional organizations in science, history, geography, foreign languages, the arts, English, and civics. The National Council of Teachers of Mathematics (NCTM) published its *Curriculum and Evaluation Standards for School Mathematics* in 1989, and in their first few years the NCTM standards were hailed as a model.[10]

SYSTEMIC REFORM

The argument for standards-based reform was articulated in an influential 1990 essay by Marshall Smith and Jennifer O'Day. Smith was dean of the Stanford Graduate School of Education, where O'Day was a PhD student. They criticized the 1980s reforms that initially responded to *A Nation at Risk* as *more of the same*: longer school days and years, more courses required for high school graduation, and more tests assessing basic skills. They characterized reform efforts that targeted individual schools as reflecting a *project mentality*, perhaps generating a few islands of success but leaving the vast educational system fragmented and incoherent. Calling for systemic school reform, Smith and O'Day urged states to take the lead by first establishing challenging standards and then integrating other state policies—assessments, accountability, teacher training, licensing, and evaluation—in line with the ambitious learning outcomes.[11]

Smith and O'Day saw systemic reform as combining the best of top-down and bottom-up approaches to school improvement. The top-down elements are easy to see; they are an updated version of the states' century-old regulation of curriculum and instruction. The bottom-up elements stem from what Smith and O'Day call *teacher professionalization*, the expertise that teachers would acquire as they shed their old-fashioned ideas about curriculum and pedagogy and learned new ways of teaching, including "a greater emphasis on complex knowledge and skills." In a later essay, Smith and O'Day elaborated on what reformed subject matter looks like: "The new reforms emphasize language- and literature-based approaches to literacy instruction, process approaches to composition, complex problem solving in mathematics, and discovery and hands-on experimentation in science."[12] In that single sentence, Smith and O'Day endorse a laundry list of progressive curricula that education traditionalists would spend most of the 1990s fighting against: whole language and balanced literacy, writing workshops, NCTM math reform, and discovery science.

State powers would increase substantially under systemic reform, especially in terms of providing "instructional guidance." By arguing that "the poor quality of U.S. curriculum and instructional practice can be attributed to the fragmented policy system," Smith and O'Day connect a curriculum that "contains little depth or coherence, emphasizing isolated facts and basic skills over opportunities to analyze and solve problems" to the dispersed nodes of policy making—federal, state, district, school, classroom—that shared authority in American education.[13] And, they argue, "It is not surprising that such curricula lead to a pedagogy that rarely demands active involvement from the learner; there are relatively few hands-on activities or group activities, few opportunities for cooperative learning, little and generally unimaginative use of computer technology, and little tolerance for activities do not have a 'right' answer or that demand sustained and imaginative problem solving."[14]

Deborah Loewenberg Ball and David K. Cohen studied the implementation of such sweeping reform and published several essays in the 1990s illuminating the difficulty of the endeavor. They noted that instructional reform emanating from state policy is inherently top-down. "An underlying assumption is that instruction is too important to be left entirely to schools and teachers: It must be closely and carefully managed by higher level agencies."[15] Changing one's teaching is not like changing an article of clothing. The ability of teachers to learn new ways of instruction is bound up with their knowledge of subject matter and ideas concerning teacher and student roles and how students learn. In responding to math reform's encouragement to use manipulatives (e.g., blocks, fraction strips), for example, Ball and Cohen observed some teachers using these tools as "another didactic agent of direct instruction" rather than a way to represent mathematical understandings or construct new knowledge. Attempting to change teaching through policy faces a conundrum: "Policies like this one are made in order to change practice, but they can only work through the practice they seek to change. Teachers are at once the targets and the agents of change."[16]

THE 1990S: SETTING STANDARDS

When Bill Clinton was elected president in 1992, he followed up on a campaign promise to establish voluntary national standards. Legislation known as Goals 2000 authorized the development of national standards that would essentially serve as a template for states in writing their own standards. States would also create assessments to measure student progress—and all of these policy tools, standards and assessments alike, would be certified by a new federal agency, the National Education Standards and Improvement Council (NESIC). Conservatives chafed at NESIC's powers of oversight, fearing that its authority to approve state standards and assessments could prove intrusive. When Republicans took control of both houses of Congress in 1996, NESIC was abolished. It disappeared not with a bang but with a whimper because it existed in name only: no member of the panel had ever been confirmed.[17]

As the standards writing projects of professional groups reached completion, they ran into political opposition. The US history standards were published in 1994 and immediately came under fire for celebrating political correctness over the story of America. Lynne V. Cheney, who served as head of the National Endowment for the Humanities from 1986 to 1993, one of the agencies funding the history standards, blasted the document in a *Wall Street Journal* op-ed, "The End of History." The first two sentences give the flavor of the critique: "Imagine an outline for the teaching of American history in which George Washington makes only a fleeting appearance and is never described as our first president. Or in which the foundings of the Sierra Club and the National Organization for Women are considered noteworthy events, but the first gathering of the U.S. Congress is not."[18] The criticism quickly became bipartisan, and within a few months, the US Senate condemned the standards by a vote of 99 to 1.

Standards in other subjects also ran into trouble. The English language arts standards, piloted by the National Council of Teachers of English and the International Reading Association, lost federal funding in 1994, but development continued with the organizations' own funds. When the standards finally were released in 1996, they were roundly criticized. The *New York Times* blasted the jargon-filled document with a review that began, "A curriculum guide for teaching English has just been released in a tongue barely recognizable as English."[19] Even the NCTM standards from 1989 fell under fire as the books and instructional materials reflecting the standards entered classrooms. Parents and professional mathematicians used a new tool for organizing grassroots movements, the internet, to criticize the NCTM standards and marshal opposition. They charged the NCTM standards with promoting "fuzzy math" and teaching children how to use calculators rather than learning the standard algorithms of arithmetic.[20]

CURRICULUM WARS: WHOLE LANGUAGE AND CONSTRUCTIVIST MATH

The philosophical conflict between progressive and traditionalist education reached a crescendo in the 1990s. In reading, policy debates featured proponents of whole language instruction versus phonics-based approaches. In math, advocates of constructivist math and traditional math argued over the content of the subject.

The whole language movement grew out of a belief that most children can learn how to read by being exposed to engaging literature. Whole language advocates oppose the exclusive use of phonics-based approaches, which teach children sounds, letter-sound relationships, and how letter-sound combinations make up words. Phonics advocates teach children to sound out words first, whereas whole language advocates stress word meaning. With whole language, the parts-to-whole orientation of phonics is reversed. When a child encounters an unfamiliar word, whole language instruction encourages strategies based on the text—taking cues from the word's use in the sentence, other words nearby, or even pictures accompanying the text—to discern the meaning. Phonics programs typically feature explicit instruction in vocabulary and comprehension.

Math reform in the late twentieth century was influenced by constructivist ideas from cognitive psychology, producing a new version of progressive, student-centered mathematics. As a pedagogical philosophy, constructivism's main idea is that students construct their own knowledge. Direct instruction by a teacher is to be avoided; teachers are "facilitators of learning rather than imparters of information." Memorizing basic arithmetic facts was out; using manipulatives to model mathematical problems was in. Paper-and-pencil, multidigit computation using standard algorithms was definitely out. The 1989 NCTM math standards referred to basic arithmetic skills as "shopkeeper arithmetic," a relic from the past and inappropriate for the modern age. Math reformer Steven Leinwand went further in 1994, arguing that "continuing to teach these skills to our students is not only unnecessary, but counterproductive and downright dangerous."[21]

John R. Anderson, Lynne M. Reder, and Herbert A. Simon of Carnegie Mellon University, who published extensive research on the cognitive processes of learning mathematics, rebutted the extreme forms of constructivism: "Modern cognitive psychology provides a basis for genuine progress by careful scientific analysis that identifies those aspects of theoretical positions that contribute to student learning and those that do not. Radical constructivism serves as the current exemplar of simplistic extremism, and certain of its devotees exhibit an anti-science bias that, should it prevail, would destroy any hope for progress in education."[22]

STANDARDS IN THE STATES

Neither the curriculum wars nor the mid-1990s controversies enveloping the national standards projects deterred states from proceeding with their own standards-based reforms. The 1994 reauthorization of the Elementary and Secondary Education Act (ESEA) provided money for states to establish standards, which most already had anyway in the name of frameworks, but it also included funds for assessments and accountability systems—the latter two components anchored to the first. By the end of the decade, forty-eight states had implemented statewide assessments. All of them tested in reading and math, but a few also tested in other subjects.[23]

Across states, the three components were not adopted uniformly. Standards varied in quality, especially in specificity and coherence. States tested students in different grades, typically once in grades 3 or 4, once in grades 7 or 8, and once in high school. Only thirteen states assessed reading and math performance every year in grades 3 through 8.[24] The greatest policy variation occurred in accountability. Researchers at the Consortium for Policy Research in Education (CPRE) surveyed the states in the 1999 to 2000 school year. The survey found that thirty-three states set performance goals for schools and districts and invoked either rewards or sanctions for meeting them; thirteen states relied simply on public reporting of scores as their primary accountability mechanism; and the remaining states allowed for locally defined accountability systems. Standards-based reform was in full bloom, but in many different varieties.[25]

Variability in state policies presents an opportunity for researchers to compare the effectiveness of approaches using quasi-experimental methods. Two studies of state accountability systems of the 1990s found positive effects on achievement. Martin Carnoy and Susanna Loeb used the CPRE results to rate state accountability policies on an index ranging from zero to five. States with stronger accountability systems were found to have made statistically significant larger gains in NAEP eighth-grade math scores from 1996 to 2000. The Carnoy and Loeb ratings included accountability targeting schools (e.g., rewards and sanctions) and accountability targeting students (e.g., passing a test to be promoted to the next grade or high school exit exams).[26]

Eric Hanushek and Margaret Raymond limited their study to school accountability and found significantly positive growth in NAEP scores for states with "consequential" accountability. Hanushek and Raymond took advantage of the fact that NAEP tests fourth and eighth graders, providing pseudocohorts in four-year intervals. The study's outcome variable was the change in NAEP reading and math scores for two cohorts, the first being between 1992 (fourth graders) and 1996 (eighth graders) and the second being between 1996 (fourth graders) and 2000 (eighth graders). Hanushek and Raymond found modest positive effects for consequential accountability on NAEP scores but no effect on closing achievement gaps between racial and ethnic groups.[27]

A study finding neutral to negative effects of accountability was published by Audrey L. Amrein and David C. Berliner in 2002. They identified eighteen states with high-stakes accountability and examined test score trends on several tests, including NAEP, but excluded state test results because of their susceptibility to manipulation. They concluded, "Evidence from this study of 18 states with high-stakes tests is that in all but one analysis, student learning is indeterminate, remains at the same level it was before the policy was implemented, or actually goes down when high-stakes testing policies are instituted."[28]

Implementation of accountability did not always go smoothly. Districts sometimes fought their state's edicts. Baltimore refused to reconstitute three schools after being ordered to do so by Maryland state officials. Los Angeles, with approximately one-fourth of its students being English language learners, sued the state of California over the requirement that state reading tests be given in English. A computer glitch led to errors in calculating 1999 test results from a leading standardized test, Terra Nova, affecting students' scores in six states. In New York City, erroneous scores led to 8,700 pupils mistakenly placed in summer school for remediation, and 3,500 of those students were wrongly forced to repeat a grade in the fall.[29]

POLITICAL OPPOSITION

Some opponents of standards rejected the whole idea, and others opposed particular state standards on the basis of curricular philosophy. One strain of general opposition came from education progressives, who objected to the loss of local educators' autonomy to decide what was best for their students, objected to the enhanced role that standards gave to testing, and especially objected to the use of test scores for high-stakes decisions. Alfie Kohn, a prodigious writer on education, traveled the country while giving talks against standards-based reform, letter grades, and the ill effects of competition in schools. Deborah Meier, the pioneering school principal from District 2 in New York City, had moved to Boston to open a school of choice, a "pilot" school, following the precepts of Ted Sizer's Coalition of Essential Schools. In 2000, Meier wrote an essay, "Educating a Democracy," which was published along with several commentaries responding to her essay in a book titled *Will Standards Save Public Education?* Meier's essential argument is that in a pluralistic, democratic society, there are multiple definitions of what constitutes a good education, and such diversity of views is a strength, not a weakness, of America's schools.[30]

At the end of the decade, Massachusetts emerged as a hot spot in the curriculum wars. In both math and English language arts, state standards with a progressive bent were rescinded in favor of traditional content. The progressive curriculum envisioned by Smith and O'Day had been pushed aside and supplanted with school subjects defined in more traditional terms. The state annually administered the Massachusetts Comprehensive Assessment System (MCAS) and used the results for both school and student accountability. Progressive educators loathed the MCAS. Meier told *Education Week*, "I have to say to parents now— and this is uncomfortable to say—'Your kids are going to be taking tests for which I do not intend to prepare them.' There's no alternative but to say that. Otherwise, we might as well close this kind of school."[31] Beginning in 2003, passing the tenth-grade MCAS was required for high school graduation. Boycotts and other forms of protest against MCAS became a new spring ritual for many Massachusetts students.[32]

Traditionalists admired the revised math and ELA standards of Massachusetts but not the standards of most states. The Fordham Foundation published scathing reviews of state ELA standards in 1997 and state math standards in 1998. The standards were described as vacuous and full of jargon, with blame laid at the feet of whole language's influence, the anti-intellectualism of national standards in ELA, and, in the case of math, the pervasive influence of the NCTM standards. But two other reviews, conducted by the American Federation of Teachers and the Council of Basic Education, were more favorable. A comparison of the three sets of reviews by *Education Week* revealed large disparities. More than half the states received ratings that differed by two letter grades in math; in English, nineteen states had such differences.[33]

Pockets of controversy regarding the content of standards should not obscure the overall picture. As a new century dawned, standards-based reform was entrenched in the states. All but two states (Iowa and Nebraska) had established state standards in reading and mathematics and administered annual tests; nearly two-thirds tied school or student consequences to test results. Variation among the states was greatest in the third component of standards-based reform, accountability, but that variability would soon come to an end.

NO CHILD LEFT BEHIND

Texas was one of the premier states with consequential accountability. After winning the 2000 election for president, Texas Governor George W. Bush brought Texas-style school reform to Washington. The reauthorization of ESEA was due, and Bush used the occasion to make the first major legislative proposal of his administration. Called the No Child Left Behind Act, the legislation wedded the cause of educational equity to standards-based reform. Bush condemned the "soft bigotry of low expectations" and advocated the disaggregation of school test scores so that the scores of Blacks, Hispanics, and other groups of historically underserved students were not hidden beneath school averages. Civil rights groups and important Democrats—including Senator Ted

Kennedy and Representative George Miller, chairs of their chambers' education committees—were won over to the legislation by a "grand bargain," which promised tough accountability provisions in exchange for increased federal funding for K–12 schools.

Republicans working on No Child Left Behind felt the existing accountability provisions in ESEA were too weak. True, states were urged to hold failing schools accountable, but the consequences were often no more than a slap on the wrist. Under NCLB, states were free to establish their own standards, develop assessments that would measure student progress, and set their own performance levels to determine what constituted *proficient* on tests. But states had little leeway in accountability. For accountability purposes, the tests had to be given annually in grades 3 to 8 and once in high school. Schools were required to demonstrate annual yearly progress (AYP) toward meeting a remarkable goal: 100 percent of students deemed proficient in reading and math by 2014. The AYP requirement applied not only to the school as a whole, but also to subgroups within schools, including racial and ethnic groups, low-income students, and those receiving special education and English language services.[34] Schools falling short of AYP for three consecutive years were subject to a series of increasingly harsh consequences, which could, if poor scores persisted, eventually lead to closure or conversion to a charter school.

NCLB passed by lopsided margins in both chambers of Congress: 381 to 41 in the House of Representatives and 87 to 10 in the Senate. As Rick Hess points out, the overwhelming support in Congress mirrored public opinion. A 1999 poll reported the following: 72 percent of the public felt that a lack of adequate standards was a problem in K–12 education; more than 90 percent believed students should have to pass a standardized test before being promoted; and 70 percent endorsed tougher standards and promotion based on test scores even if "significantly more" students were held back.[35]

President Bush signed NCLB into law in January 2002, and its testing provisions were immediately activated. States established baseline performance for schools using test data from the 2001–2002 school year, from which AYP calculations were made. The popularity of NCLB, like all standards-based reforms, probably reached its apogee on the day the bill was signed into law. Standards are aspirational. Local schools are loved by their communities; accountability is for failing schools located elsewhere. The utopian goal of attaining universal student proficiency in reading and math had been placed far enough into the future that even in 2004, after a couple of years of NCLB's implementation, public support for high standards remained strong.

But tiny fissures were soon apparent. As Hess notes, support for high standards did not mean the public embraced NCLB's regime of escalating sanctions. A 2002 PDK/Gallup poll found that 77 percent of respondents supported giving low-performing schools more money (with 22 percent opposed), while the idea of closing schools identified as *needing improvement* was rejected by a similar margin, with only 21 percent supporting and 77 percent opposed. Even in NCLB's early years, trying to fix, rather than punish, schools was the public's preferred remedy for low achievement.

CONCLUSION

The rise of the standards movement at the end of the twentieth century featured fully evolved aspects of state authority that were born a century earlier. States had built out the inchoate state education departments of the early twentieth century into full-fledged regulatory agencies. That doesn't mean these agencies could directly control what transpired in classrooms—no more than agricultural agencies grow crops or transportation agencies fly planes or drive train or bus routes—but they could set standards, administer tests, and sanction schools and students based on test results.

Both eras featured famous commission reports that declared schools were failing, not focused on the right kinds of knowledge, or doing too little to stay up with modern times—documents that catalyzed school reform movements. Expertise grew in importance. In both eras, scholars who studied the increasingly sophisticated fields of curriculum and instruction included experts evangelizing fundamental reform. When practitioners or the public resisted, the reformers insisted that expertise should trump democracy, that science should trump public sentiments. Thomas Timar points out that many of the early twentieth-century reforms were policy initiatives that emanated from education progressives, not from the public.[36]

The public did not clamor for the curriculum reforms of the late twentieth century either. In fact, one prestigious panel that issued a 1995 report on standards-based reform warned against allowing public input to override professional judgment: "Standards resulting from such a process will not only be weak pedagogically, but will also almost inevitably reflect past practices rather than reform goals; that is, they will reflect those approaches to knowledge and skills that parents and the general adult population experienced in their own schooling and with which they are therefore comfortable." The report is clear on where final authority should rest: "The Panel thus concludes that while public involvement is valuable and necessary to the acceptance and long term viability of new content standards, the responsibility for guaranteeing that those standards present a coherent, up-to-date and challenging vision of a field of study ultimately resides with the professionals engaged in ongoing work in that knowledge domain." [37]

As we have seen, policies are often predicated on previous policies, either standing in opposition to previous policies or trying to fix their deficiencies. The state mandates set immediately after the release of *A Nation at Risk* explicitly rejected the previous era's laissez-faire policy of allowing local schools and districts to set their own high school graduation requirements. The goal was to restore the legitimacy of a high school diploma by certifying at least minimum competency in school subjects. The standards of the 1990s were meant to provide cognitively challenging content, in contrast to the earlier policies' emphasis on minimum competency and basic skills. The No Child Left Behind Act toughened up the accountability provisions of ESEA, taking away state discretion on how to deal with schools persistently falling short on state tests. From each of these efforts, authority over curriculum and instruction flowed upward, away from local schools and districts to state—and even federal—governments.

Despite the trend toward centralization, upper-level authority is constrained. Cohen and Ball's point that instructional reform positions teachers as both the targets and agents of reform echoes the findings of earlier studies of implementation. Evaluating the effect of a full decade of federal education programs that promoted innovation, Paul Berman and Milbrey McLaughlin coined the term *mutual adaptation* in the 1970s to describe what happens to policy when it reaches schools and classrooms. Even if a policy succeeds in changing practice, it, too, may be changed by practitioners who adapt policies in accord with individual circumstances. "Each classroom, each school, and each school system, being somewhat different from the others," they explain, "implements the same innovations in different ways at different times or places."[38] Richard Elmore elaborates on the same phenomenon by detailing the limitations even school principals face in standardizing teaching over dozens of classrooms, citing it as evidence of "the power of the bottom over the top."[39]

The next chapter includes the ending to the NCLB story. A discussion of NCLB's shortcomings and the law's eventual unpopularity will illuminate what the authors of Common Core hoped to accomplish—and some of the pitfalls they hoped to avoid.

3

DEVELOPING THE
COMMON CORE
STATE STANDARDS

No Child Left Behind contained within it a ticking time bomb. The accountability system that could eventually close failing schools was based on goals for student learning in 2014. By June of the 2013–2014 school year, all students were supposed to score as proficient on state tests in reading and math. The deadline seemed far off in the early years, but as time passed, it grew uncomfortably closer. When states originally established adequate yearly progress schedules for schools, about half opted for *backloading*—invoking lenient expectations in the first few years, and then ramping them up.[1] By the middle of the first decade of the 2000s, it was time for the curve to steepen. More and more students would have to score proficient on state tests, including English language learners, special education students, and the other major subgroups at each school. Otherwise, schools would be declared in need of improvement and subject to NCLB sanctions.

Discontent with NCLB was growing. Complaints came from teachers and parents about too much testing, too much test prep, and narrowing of the curriculum to only content that was tested.[2] Academics argued that accountability should focus on achievement growth rather than status. In other words, they recommended rewarding or sanctioning schools based on the gains students made during a school year, not on the percentage of students scoring as proficient. A school that succeeded in raising the number of proficient students from 20 percent to 50 percent could arguably be considered more successful than a school in which proficiency dropped from 90 percent to 80 percent, and yet the former would be considered failing under NCLB and the latter would not.

NCLB RESEARCH

It is difficult to conduct a sound evaluation of policies such as NCLB. National policies leave no states to form a comparison group. Thomas Dee and Brian Jacob got around that problem by comparing states that already had accountability systems when NCLB was adopted to those that did not. As noted earlier, about half of the states had some sort of consequential accountability system before NCLB. Dee and Jacob created a policy variable that accounted for the number of years those systems operated. For the states without accountability before NCLB, 2003 was set as their first "treated" year. In a method known as *comparative interrupted time series analysis*, the change in trends of these two groups are compared to distill the effect of the treatment—which in this case is NCLB accountability. Dee and Jacob extended the analysis back to the early 1990s and gathered state NAEP scores and information on accountability policies for 1992 to 2007.[3]

The two grades and two subjects of NAEP create four reporting categories: fourth-grade math, fourth-grade reading, eighth-grade math, and eighth-grade reading. Dee and Jacob found positive—and statistically significant—results in fourth-grade math (an effect size of 0.23 in student-level standard deviations) and nearly significant results in eighth-grade math (an effect size of 0.10). No significant effects were found in either fourth- or eighth-grade reading. Manyee Wong, Thomas Cook, and Peter Steiner also analyzed state NAEP scores to estimate NCLB's effects. They used the number of schools in danger of receiving NCLB sanctions from 2003 to 2011 as the NCLB policy variable. They found positive effects in both fourth- and eighth-grade math and "consistent but statistically weak evidence of a possible, but distinctly smaller, fourth grade reading effect." No effect was detected in eighth-grade reading.[4]

It's important to stress that both of these studies evaluated a single element of NCLB, test-based accountability, rather than the entire law. Neither study attempted to evaluate the quality of the content standards adopted by states.

RACE TO THE BOTTOM?

An important line of criticism of NCLB helped set the stage for Common Core. As noted in the previous chapter, states used the NAEP term *proficient* to set achievement goals for schools on state tests. States crafted their own tests and set cut points for what constituted proficient wherever they liked. But states also participated in NAEP, and it had its own, quite lofty cut points for proficiency. Several analysts compared the percentage of students scoring proficient on state tests with the percentage scoring proficient on state NAEP tests. This set off alarms. States consistently reported more students as proficient on their own tests, some by wide margins. In 2014, for example, Georgia reported more than 90 percent of its fourth graders proficient in reading, but on the 2013 NAEP test, fewer than 40 percent of the state's fourth graders scored proficient. The implication was that states were fudging the data and presenting a grossly distorted picture of how well students were learning.

In 2006, in an article in *Education Next*, Paul Peterson and coauthors began giving states grades by comparing state and NAEP proficiency rates, explaining that allowing states to define proficient performance on their own tests "has led to the bizarre situation in which some states achieve handsome proficiency results by grading their students against low standards, while other states suffer poor proficiency ratings only because they have high standards."[5]

The labels *high standards* and *low standards* are important here because they are being used in a particular manner. The terms mean different things when applied in different contexts. Content standards in math, reading, science, or history define what states are urging schools to teach. Common Core is a set of content standards. The *Education Next* review grades states based on *performance* standards, the level of student learning that states deem acceptable. States with high standards are those with a higher bar for proficiency on their state tests, irrespective of the standards defining the content of school subjects. From this point of view, states could have math standards that taught bad mathematics, but if their tests identified a similar number of proficient students as NAEP, those states would be seen as having high standards. To appreciate the difference, consider that one of *Education Next*'s institutional sponsors, the Thomas B. Fordham Foundation (known as the Thomas B. Fordham Institute after 2007), periodically published reviews of state content standards. The Fordham Foundation was founded and led for many years by Chester E. Finn Jr., also an executive editor of *Education Next*. Of the six states receiving As in *Education Next*'s 2006 ratings of math *performance* standards, five received Ds or Fs in the Fordham Foundation's 2005 review of math *content* standards: the District of Columbia (D), Maine (D), Missouri (F), South Carolina (D), and Wyoming (F). A high bar for proficient test performance does not always equal good content.

A study by the National Center for Education Statistics (NCES) mapped the state thresholds for proficiency onto the NAEP scale. By comparing the states' proficient cut points for reading and math in 2005 and 2007—and in both fourth and eighth grades—the study found that some states had lowered the proficiency bar. In a story headlined "Federal Researchers Find Lower Standards in Schools," the *New York Times* summarized the study as follows: "It found that 15 states lowered their proficiency standards in fourth- or eighth-grade reading or math from 2005 to 2007. Three states, Maine, Oklahoma and Wyoming, lowered standards in both subjects at both grade levels, the study said. Eight states increased the rigor of their standards in one or both subjects and grades. Some states raised standards in one subject but lowered them in another, including New York, which raised the rigor of its fourth-grade-math standard but lowered the standard in eighth-grade reading, the study said."[6] The article included a response from US Secretary of Education Arne Duncan: "At a time when we should be raising standards to compete in the global economy, more states are lowering the bar than raising it. We're lying to our children." Duncan would later cite these data to accuse states of "dummying down" standards.

The actual results of the NCES study are less dramatic and less damning than either Duncan or the *New York Times* headline implies. Of the 146 comparisons of 2005 and 2007 proficiency bars, more than half of the states (52 percent) made no significant change. It's true that states that made changes were twice as likely to lower the bar rather than to raise it, but that is largely an eighth-grade phenomenon (see table 3.1). At the fourth-grade level, the number of states that raised cut points (nine in reading and seven in math) were nearly the same as the number of states that lowered them (seven in reading and ten in math).

TABLE 3.1   *Number of states raising and lowering bar for scoring proficient on state tests, 2005–2007*

	TOTAL NUMBER OF STATES	RAISED BAR	LOWERED BAR	NO SIGNIFICANT CHANGE
Fourth-grade reading	34	9 (26%)	7 (21%)	18 (53%)
Fourth-grade math	35	7 (20%)	10 (29%)	18 (51%)
Eighth-grade reading	38	3 (8%)	15 (39%)	20 (53%)
Eighth-grade math	39	4 (10%)	15 (38%)	20 (51%)
Total	**146**	**23 (16%)**	**47 (32%)**	**76 (52%)**

Source: Author, based on data from tables 11–12 and 17–18 in Victor Bandeira de Mello, Charles Blankenship, and Don McLaughlin, *Mapping State Proficiency Standards onto NAEP Scales: 2005–2007* (Washington, DC: National Center for Education Statistics, 2009).

Comparing proficiency on state tests to proficiency on NAEP comes with a number of caveats. The state tests have stakes for students; NAEP does not. Studies show that students can score significantly higher when even modest rewards are offered to students before taking a low-stakes test. For example, a twenty-dollar reward resulted in a 0.12 to 0.20 standard deviation improvement in a Chicago experiment with high school students.[7] An experiment with American and Shanghai students found rewards boosted Americans' PISA scores by 22 to 24 points (about 0.22–0.24 standard deviation), but had no effect on the Chinese students' scores.[8] Passing a state test may be required for student grade promotion or graduation. Schools face consequences for low scores on state tests. NAEP does not even produce student- or school-level scores. Comparing results on high- and low-stakes tests is not an apples-to-apples comparison.

The evidence is thin that NAEP proficiency is where proficiency cut points should be placed. NAEP has four performance levels: below basic, basic, proficient, and advanced. When the performance standards were released in the early 1990s, the US General Accounting Office (GAO), National Research Council, and the National Academy of Education published highly critical reviews questioning the validity of the standards.[9] The National Research Council's report called the standards *fundamentally flawed*. The GAO pointed out evidence suggesting that the cut point for proficiency seemed too high to serve as a legitimate indicator of college readiness and, after examining licensure tests, concluded that even the basic performance category might be too high as an indicator of successful entry into several occupations.[10]

Longitudinal data collected from 1992 high school seniors found that about half (49.5 percent) of students scoring at NAEP's basic level in twelfth-grade math in 1992 went on to earn a bachelor degree by 2000. For students scoring proficient, a whopping 79 percent went on to earn a bachelor degree.[11] That's an extremely lofty standard to expect of every student. Only about 10 percent of the class of 1992 took a calculus course in high school, and that group's rate of later completing a bachelor degree was 83 percent, comparable to the NAEP proficient group.[12]

According to the Organisation for Economic Co-operation and Development (OECD), Canada had the highest completion rate for tertiary education in 2018 at 56 percent, which includes two-year degrees. The United States ranked sixth at 46 percent.[13] Consider that today's forty-year-olds have earned more college diplomas than any generation in American history, with about 40 percent holding a four-year degree. But on the NAEP eighth-grade test given in 1992—when they were about thirteen years old and in eighth grade—only 29 percent scored proficient in ELA and 15 percent in math. NAEP proficient is too stringent to accurately predict college graduation, let alone less lofty outcomes that are beneficial for a productive adulthood, such as gaining college admission and completing some college without getting a degree, graduation from a two-year college, or success at a skilled occupation not requiring a degree.[14] One need not score at the NAEP proficient level to stand a good chance at achieving one of those accomplishments. The percentage of students scoring as basic is a more reasonable standard of success—and importantly, the percentage scoring below basic is a strong indicator of the need for interventions to remediate learning difficulties.

NCLB'S FALLING POLL NUMBERS

The irony is that at the same time NCLB was coming under fire for expecting schools to achieve a utopian goal, universal proficiency by 2014, it was also coming under fire for allowing states to create their own standards and tests—and to define student proficiency in math and reading as they liked. Critics charged that NCLB was either too rigorous in its goals, asking for schools to do the impossible, or not rigorous enough in implementation, allowing states to give a false picture of progress.

The pivotal year in public opinion of NCLB was 2007. Approval flipped. The PDK/Gallup poll found 40 percent of respondents with a negative view of NCLB, compared to 31 percent favorable. The previous year's split was 32 percent favorable to 31 percent unfavorable.[15] Representative George Miller summed up NCLB's public relations problem with these words: "At the end of the day, it may be the most tainted brand in America."[16]

It did not help that NCLB was associated with George W. Bush, who, as his second term wound down, was a profoundly unpopular president. In addition, the tick of the accountability time bomb was growing louder. A study by the Center on Education Policy released in September 2008 estimated that over 3,500 schools had fallen under NCLB's restructuring sanction in 2007–2008, an increase of more than 50 percent from the previous year.[17] When the Bush administration departed and the Obama administration entered office in January 2009, the country was in a deep recession. School districts were laying off teachers and curtailing all but the most essential services. The reauthorization of ESEA was due in 2008, but that was an election year. Congress made no progress on legislation.

In December 2008, three organizations—National Governors Association (NGA), Council of Chief State School Officers (CCSSO), and Achieve, Inc.—released *Benchmarking for Success: Ensuring U.S. Students Receive a World-Class Education*. The report called on states to take five actions. The first was to adopt a "common core of internationally benchmarked standards in math and language arts for grades K–12"; the second was to align textbooks, curricula, and assessments to the standards.[18] The other three actions involved teacher licensure, performance standards on tests, and accountability—all to be aligned with the standards and benchmarked internationally so that students were "globally competitive." The document urged states to adopt the standards of the Common Core State Standards Initiative, noting that it was a project in the planning stages. The standards had not been written yet.[19]

GATES WRITES A CHECK

State education leaders met in Chicago in April 2009. The CCSSO and NGA convened the meeting and presented participants with a three-page memorandum of understanding (MOU). The representatives were to take the MOU back to state school chiefs and governors for consideration. By signing the MOU, states committed to taking part in the development of a common core of standards in English language arts and mathematics in grades K–12, but not necessarily to adopt them. Forty-eight states would eventually sign the MOU.[20]

The prior summer, Gene Wilhoit of CCSSO, and the cofounder and CEO of Student Achievement Partners, David Coleman, met with Bill and Melinda Gates. They outlined a Common Core project and asked the Gateses for their foundation's support. Wilhoit and Coleman argued that with fifty separate state standards, a high school diploma meant meeting a separate set of accomplishments from state to state. The fragmentation stifled innovation. Instead of crafting new materials to sell to a large, unified customer base, publishers and other producers of curricula had to cater to small, disparate markets. According to the *Washington Post*, Gates asked Wilhoit if he could guarantee that states would participate in the project. Wilhoit responded that there were no guarantees but that he and Coleman would do all that they could to see that it happened. After the meeting broke up, Wilhoit and Coleman heard nothing for several weeks. Then the phone call came: Gates agreed to support Common Core.[21]

The Bill & Melinda Gates Foundation eventually spent more than $200 million financing the development of Common Core, a vast political network to promote state adoption of the standards, and a public relations effort to fend off political opposition. The MOU showed that Wilhoit and Coleman had upheld their promise by getting at least preliminary commitments from all but a couple of states.[22]

WRITING COMMON CORE

Writing the standards was conducted in two phases. First, drawing heavily on an existing set of college readiness standards from the American Diploma Project, representatives from Achieve, ACT, and the College Board codified the math and ELA outcomes that the standards intended students to achieve by the end of high school. What should a graduating senior know in math and ELA to be college and career ready? College and career readiness was defined as able to enter college without needing to take remedial classes. These standards were vetted by an advisory panel and posted for public comment. Using the college and career readiness standards as an endpoint, the writing committees in the two subjects then proceeded to backward map grade-level standards all the way back to kindergarten. These were also released for public comment. Approximately ten thousand comments were received, and the draft was revised. The final step was a review of the final draft of the standards by a validation committee of academics, policymakers, and educators attesting that the standards complied with research and were comparable to the expectations of high-performing nations.[23]

The English language arts writing team was headed by David Coleman, cofounder of Student Achievement Partners, an education company, and Susan Pimentel, cofounder of Standards Works. The leads for the math standards were William McCallum, a math professor at the University of Arizona; Phillip Daro of America's Choice; and Jason Zimba, who taught mathematics and physics at Bennington College, but was also the other cofounder of Student Achievement Partners with Coleman. Before Student Achievement Partners, he and Coleman founded an education technology company in 2000 called Grow Network, offering tools to help schools and districts use standardized test data. They sold that company to McGraw-Hill in 2004.[24]

The lead writers had extensive experience with K–12 standards and consulting but not with K–12 teaching. The lack of classroom teachers' participation in the development of the CCSS became a flashpoint for critics of the standards, as did the amount of development that was conducted behind closed doors.[25] The conventional process for writing K–12 standards typically meant convening a large group of teachers and administrators representing particular grades, dividing into smaller writing teams to write standards for a small number of grades, and then collating all of the parts into a whole document. After a small number of experienced standards writers smoothed the document into coherence, a draft of the standards would appear for public comment and often would be presented in public hearings. After several months of public vetting and input from educators, a final draft was prepared.

The architects of Common Core believed that the states' standards-writing process led to bloated standards that included everything and left nothing out. Asking for the input of hundreds of educators, and then favoring the inclusion of ideas over their exclusion, was bound to produce bulky standards. Coleman and Zimba had written a paper in 2007 that called for fewer, clearer, higher standards, and that became the mantra of Common Core.[26] One of the main justifications for less than full transparency involves politics. The Common Core founders were determined to avoid the political turmoil that engulfed national standards in the 1990s. They wished to avoid instigating a flare-up in the math wars or battles over whole language, the most recent manifestations of a century-long conflict over pedagogy between education progressives and traditionalists. As the CCSS were being written, Sean Cavanaugh reported in *Education Week*: "A number of participants in the last major movement to write voluntary national academic standards, during the 1990s, described those processes as more open than the one going on today. But those observers also noted that the former efforts, which played out across different subjects and were in some cases underwritten by the federal government, took several years and were marked by strong divisions over curriculum and content."[27]

Critics charged that development of the standards was rushed. The final version of the CCSS was released on June 2, 2010, less than fourteen months after the initial Chicago meeting with state officials. That is a remarkably fast timeline from inception to completion for standards. Even more astonishing, the draft of the standards for public comment was released on March 10, 2010. The comment period was open until April 2, nearly ten thousand comments were received, and they were processed and incorporated into a final, publishable draft within sixty days. Catherine Gewertz of *Education Week* reported that two thousand comments were submitted in the first nine days, also noting that only a summary of the comments would be made public, not the comments themselves.[28] The summary was released on the same day as the standards, June 2, 2010, along with the report from the validation committee.

The conduct of the validation committee also fueled criticism. When the report of the committee was released, twenty-four of the original members were listed as signing the report. Five members did not agree to the validation. One was Dylan Wiliam. Four years later, Wiliam explained on Rick Hess's *Education Week* blog why he didn't formally sign-off on CCSS. The signatories were asked to attest that the CCSS were

1. reflective of the core knowledge and skills in ELA and mathematics that students need to be college and career ready;
2. appropriate in terms of their level of clarity and specificity;
3. comparable to the expectations of other leading nations;
4. informed by available research or evidence;
5. the result of processes that reflect best practices for standards development;
6. a solid starting point for adoption of cross state common core standards; and
7. a sound basis for eventual development of standards-based assessments.

Wiliam's email response to the project directors included the following:

> I have been wrestling with this for the last couple of days. I can agree with statements 1, 6 and 7. I can persuade myself that statements 4 and 5 are just about OK (although it's a stretch). However, I cannot in all conscience, endorse statements 2 and 3. The standards are, in my view, much more detailed, and, as Jim Milgram has pointed out, are in important respects less demanding, than the standards of the leading nations. For this reason, while I can see there are strong political reasons for securing consensus, and while I can see that they are the best that we can get at this stage, I am unable to agree to "sign off" on the standards if doing so is taken to be assent to all 7 propositions.[29]

Two of the most vocal dissenters were W. James Milgram, professor emeritus of mathematics at Stanford University, and Sandra Stotsky, professor in the Department of Education Reform at the University of Arkansas. Milgram had served as a primary author of California's 1997 math standards and subsequently worked with a number of states on their math standards. Before joining the faculty at the University of Arkansas, Stotsky served as a senior associate commissioner in the Massachusetts Department of Education, where she headed the state's standards-writing efforts. Milgram and Stotsky both support standards and are education traditionalists. Their rejection of Common Core was based on the process that produced the standards and the content of the math and ELA standards.

Stotsky charged that the validation committee was "useless" and no more than a rubber stamp. The committee only met twice, and committee members signed nondisclosure agreements for what was discussed. Stotsky complained that the committee requested citations for the research supporting the claim that the standards were informed by research or evidence (statement 4 in the earlier list), but none were provided.[30] She points out that the initial ELA work team included no high school English teacher, nor a college English professor, two groups that would be presumed to possess expertise concerning college readiness.

THE FEDERAL ROLE

On June 14, 2009, less than two months after the Chicago meeting that launched the Common Core, Arne Duncan, US secretary of education, spoke to the 2009 Governors Education Symposium. Duncan gave a rousing endorsement of the Common Core initiative:

> Gene Wilhoit has made national standards his top priority as the executive director of the Council of Chief State School Officers. Thanks to his organization and the NGA (National Governors Association). Your hard work and leadership are paying off. As I said before, 46 states and three territories have now committed to creating common internationally benchmarked college- and career-ready standards. And you deserve a big, big hand for that. Creating common standards hasn't always been popular. Right now, though, there's a growing consensus that this is the right thing to do.[31]

Duncan went on to briefly mention a new competition for federal money. The Obama administration's Race to the Top program offered states $4.4 billion in funds. States competed for the money by submitting reform plans covering four areas, with adoption of internationally benchmarked college and career readiness standards mentioned first. Promising to implement teacher evaluation systems linked to standards-based test scores was another important Race to the Top component. The deadline to apply for Phase 1 was January 19, 2010, and states had to promise to approve qualifying standards by August 2, 2010, to receive bonus points in the competition. The standards did not have to be the CCSS but having signed the MOU regarding CCSS was acceptable as verification of commitment. Forty states and the District of Columbia applied. All but one committed to adopting CCSS.[32]

After the standards were released in June 2010, the states had less than two months before the Race to the Top deadline. Kentucky officials had already adopted the CCSS earlier in the year, based on drafts they had seen of the standards. In May, Hawaii, Maryland, and West Virginia followed suit and adopted CCSS before the standards had been finalized. After the June release, state adoption shifted into high gear: thirteen states adopted CCSS in June, and fourteen states and the District of Columbia in July.[33] The recession was deepening, and states were desperate for revenue. In September 2010, the Department of Education announced grants to two consortia to produce assessments aligned to CCSS: Partnership for Assessment of Readiness for College and Careers (PARCC), and Smarter Balanced Assessment Consortium. Conservative critics of CCSS pointed to Secretary Duncan's frequent praise of Common Core, Race to the Top's ties to CCSS, and federal funding of the assessment consortia as evidence of federal government overreach.

The adoptions in California and Massachusetts stand out for pushback against Common Core. As pointed out in the previous chapter, both states had existing academic standards that received high ratings from outside groups. A decade earlier, both states experienced fierce battles between progressive curriculum reformers and traditionalists. ELA standards that were accused of being pro whole language or vague on content and math standards that were criticized for supporting NCTM-style math reform were overturned and replaced with more traditional standards. Stotsky and Milgram participated in both states' curriculum debates. Stotsky still sat on the Massachusetts state board of education when it approved the CCSS after a "fiery debate" in July 2010.[34] California's academic standards commission approved CCSS in late July, just in the nick of time to qualify for Race to the Top bonus points and after hearing the vigorous dissent of two former Department of Education officials who served under George W. Bush, Bill Evers and Ze'ev Wurman.[35]

CONCLUSION

Common Core represents a policy viewed favorably by the public. The idea of common national standards and tests has been around a long time. A 1989 Gallup poll found that 69 percent of the public favored a "standardized national curriculum" and 77 percent endorsed testing students to see if they met the standards.[36] Two decades later, as NCLB began to flounder, a powerful coalition of policy elites came together to take advantage of the moment. To use political scientist John Kingdon's term, a *policy window* had opened and the time was ripe for political action. An important aspect of Kingdon's theories on how proposals rise to the top of the policy agenda is that solutions often precede the problems they are designed to solve, sitting innocuously on a shelf, perhaps for several years—even decades—until advocates believe an opportune time has arrived to push them forward.[37]

Common Core advocates had learned several lessons from the failures of NCLB and previous standards-based policies. Of the two most important, first, the standards must be seen as national in the sense of a multistate effort, not policy emanating from the federal government. Common Core advocates learned early on to stress that CCSS were *state* standards. The second lesson was that every effort must be made to navigate the treacherous politics of standards: try to satisfy both progressives and traditionalists in order to tamp down their ancient wars over curriculum and pedagogy, and favor quick completion and adoption of the standards over an endless process that solicits and incorporates public input.

As was true with NCLB a decade earlier, Common Core probably hit its zenith in popularity shortly after adoption. A 2011 poll commissioned by Achieve found widespread support for the basic argument animating CCSS: the need for common standards and tests across states, instead of allowing states to go their own way. The poll also found that 60 percent of voters reported knowing "nothing" about CCSS and 21 percent indicated they knew "not much."[38]

A strong political coalition supported CCSS. Political conservatives, such as former Florida Governor Jeb Bush, former US Secretary of Education William Bennett, and the Thomas B. Fordham Institute, supported standards and assessments as anchors for accountability systems—especially if the systems graded schools and produced tougher evaluation of teachers—along with the political right's usual menu of choice-based policies: vouchers, charter schools, and education savings accounts,. Political liberals (Education Trust, Center for American Progress, teachers' unions, civil rights groups) bought into standards as a tool for promoting equity. Black, Hispanic, and disadvantaged children would finally be exposed to the knowledge and skills that were taught in leafy suburbs.

Another group of CCSS supporters contained educators focused on the standards' promise of what they could offer to improve the K–12 curriculum. The two national teachers' unions, the National Education Association (NEA) and the American Federation of Teachers (AFT), embraced the standards. Education progressives such as Jo Boaler, Linda Darling Hammond, Steven Leinwand, and Lucy Calkins supported CCSS. The Partnership for 21st Century Skills praised the CCSS for emphasizing higher-order thinking, communication skills, deeper learning, and other nontraditional learning outcomes. Some traditionalists who saw progressive pedagogy as a means of dodging content and knowledge were alarmed at elements of CCSS, but they made their stand in California and Massachusetts and lost. Other notable traditionalists, such as E. D. Hirsch of Core Knowledge fame, backed Common Core. He believed the standards offered the potential for instruction in the fields of literature, history, science, and the arts, the traditional liberal arts subjects.

And providing funding to all of the CCSS supporters was Bill Gates and the Bill & Melinda Gates Foundation. As the battle to adopt CCSS morphed into a national campaign to see the standards faithfully implemented, the Gates Foundation, according to Mercedes K. Schneider, awarded grants to 165 organizations.[39]

This was a powerful coalition, but it was fragile. The coalition partners had their differences. Accountability hawks were opposed by teachers' unions, especially if teacher evaluations were tied to the standards. The progressive-traditionalist battles over curriculum and pedagogy had existed for over a century and seemed never to go away. As the field of play for CCSS shifted from debates over state adoption to implementation, states began working with districts and schools to make the standards a reality in classrooms.

After the midterm elections of 2010, Republicans controlled more state legislative seats than at any time since 1928. The election featured a new political force, the Tea Party movement, which was distrustful of CCSS.[40] Nevertheless, standards and accountability were high on the public's list of favored school reforms, and CCSS enjoyed bipartisan support. The 2011 Education Next Poll reaffirmed that support the following year:

> Breaking from existing law, however, Americans support the creation of a single national test in both reading and math. Under No Child Left Behind, each state develops its own test and benchmarks for determining student proficiency. Solid pluralities of both the general public and all subgroups, however, believe that there should be one test and one standard for all students across the country. Roughly one in five, by contrast, supports different tests and standards in different states. A paltry number of respondents think that all state and federal tests should be abolished.[41]

Common Core was riding high. As we will see in the next two chapters, that did not last long.

4

CONTENT OF
THE CORE

Common Core State Standards for English Language Arts & Literacy in History/Social Studies, Science, and Technical Subjects includes standards for reading, writing, speaking and listening, and language. Reading standards for literature and informational text are provided for grades K–5 and 6–12. Standards for foundational skills in reading (e.g., phonics, decoding, and fluency) are provided for K–5. The standards for literacy in history/social studies, science, and technical subjects cover grades 6–12. The entire document is sixty-six pages long. Three appendices are also available. Appendix A supplies research supporting the standards; appendix B contains a list of exemplary texts and sample performance tasks; and appendix C offers student writing samples.

Common Core State Standards for Mathematics consists of content standards for K–8, along with content standards for three high school courses and eight standards for mathematical practice. The K–8 content standards are organized by clusters (groups of related standards) and domains (math topics). The high school standards are presented by conceptual categories: number and quantity, algebra, functions, modeling, geometry, and statistics and probability, with the intention of serving either traditional (Algebra I, Geometry, and Algebra II) or integrated (Mathematics I, Mathematics II, and Mathematics III) course sequences in grades 9–11.[1] The document covers ninety-three pages. Appendix A provides more information on how the high school standards can be organized within both traditional and integrated course sequences.

A STRENGTH OF THE MATH STANDARDS: RESTORING THE IMPORTANCE OF ARITHMETIC

Arithmetic was the main topic of elementary grade mathematics throughout most of the twentieth century. As mentioned in chapter 2, the 1989 NCTM math standards were influential in diminishing the preeminence of arithmetic, installing instead five strands of content for K–12 mathematics: number and operations (under which arithmetic was subsumed), algebra, geometry, measurement, and data analysis and probability. These five content strands were adopted by the National Assessment Governing Board, the board that oversees NAEP, as the content assessed by NAEP in grades 4, 8, and 12. They also became the topics under which most states established math standards in the 1990s.[2]

Thomas Romberg, chair of the NCTM standards project, argued: "Today, no one makes a living doing shopkeeper arithmetic. Instead, we need for students to understand a lot about calculation—not necessarily to be good at calculation—and be able to use the technology to do more complex calculations than could ever be done by paper and pencil."[3]

The official embrace of the NCTM standards by officials in both Washington, DC, and the states was a great victory for progressive math reformers. Calculators were in, starting in kindergarten; pencil and paper calculations were out. The emphasis was particularly devastating to the study of fractions. As Ralph A. Raimi and Lawrence Braden state in their 1998 review of state math standards, "The NCTM officially prescribes the early use of calculators with an enthusiasm the authors of this report deplore, and the NCTM discourages the memorization of certain elementary processes such as 'long division' of decimally expressed real numbers and the pencil and paper arithmetic of all fractions, that we think essential, and that should be second nature *before* the calculator is invoked for practical uses."[4]

FRACTIONS AS NUMBERS

Despite disagreeing on instructional strategies for teaching fractions, progressives and traditionalists agree that fractions are one of the most important and difficult concepts children learn in elementary math. Cognitive psychologist Robert S. Siegler and colleagues have conducted studies showing that knowledge of fractions is a good predictor of how well students do when they move on to the study of advanced mathematics such as algebra in high school. The statistical association holds up even after controlling for socioeconomic and cognitive characteristics, including general math skills.[5] Fractions are typically introduced with visual representations of fractions in part-whole relationships: half of an apple, one-fourth of a pizza, and so on. These models are okay but are limited. Students need to see fractions as numbers, not as pizza slices, or difficulties will surface when working with anything beyond the simplest fraction.

CCSS starts the teaching of fractions in third grade with a cluster of standards. Right off the bat, students are asked to understand fractions as numbers, with the number line used to illustrate the concept. Note that third grade work with fractions is limited to fractions with denominators of 2, 3, 4, 6, and 8. Readers who locate the standards online will see the following:

Develop understanding of fractions as numbers.

CCSS.Math.Content.3.NF.A.1

Understand a fraction $1/b$ as the quantity formed by 1 part when a whole is partitioned into b equal parts; understand a fraction a/b as the quantity formed by a parts of size $1/b$.[6]

CCSS.Math.Content.3.NF.A.2

Understand a fraction as a number on the number line; represent fractions on a number line diagram.[7]

CCSS.Math.Content.3.NF.A.2.a

Represent a fraction $1/b$ on a number line diagram by defining the interval from 0 to 1 as the whole and partitioning it into b equal parts. Recognize that each part has size $1/b$ and that the endpoint of the part based at 0 locates the number $1/b$ on the number line.[8]

CCSS.Math.Content.3.NF.A.2.b

Represent a fraction a/b on a number line diagram by marking off a lengths $1/b$ from 0. Recognize that the resulting interval has size a/b and that its endpoint locates the number a/b on the number line.[9]

CCSS.Math.Content.3.NF.A.3
Explain equivalence of fractions in special cases, and compare fractions by reasoning about their size.[10]

CCSS.Math.Content.3.NF.A.3.a
Understand two fractions as equivalent (equal) if they are the same size, or the same point on a number line.[11]

CCSS.Math.Content.3.NF.A.3.b
Recognize and generate simple equivalent fractions, e.g., 1/2 = 2/4, 4/6 = 2/3. Explain why the fractions are equivalent, e.g., by using a visual fraction model.[12]

CCSS.Math.Content.3.NF.A.3.c
Express whole numbers as fractions, and recognize fractions that are equivalent to whole numbers. *Examples: Express 3 in the form 3 = 3/1; recognize that 6/1 = 6; locate 4/4 and 1 at the same point of a number line diagram.*[13]

CCSS.Math.Content.3.NF.A.3.d
Compare two fractions with the same numerator or the same denominator by reasoning about their size. Recognize that comparisons are valid only when the two fractions refer to the same whole. Record the results of comparisons with the symbols >, =, or <, and justify the conclusions, e.g., by using a visual fraction model.[14]

See http://www.corestandards.org/Math/Content/3/NF/

This is a lot of content. For readers who would like to get into the weeds of how the standards fit together across grade levels, let me explain how CCSS standards are coded. There are three standards: 3.NF.A.1, 3.NF.A.2, and 3.NF.A.3, with the second branching into two sub-standards, showing ways of representing fractions on a number line, and the third branching into four sub-standards, demonstrating fraction equivalence. The notation 3.NF indicates that the standard is from the third grade for the *domain* of Number and Operations-Fractions. A reader can track the flow of standards pertaining to fractions from grade to grade by following the domain; for example, fourth-grade fractions standards begin with 4.NF, fifth grade with 5.NF, and so on. The A after NF designates the *cluster* in which the standard resides—in this case, "Develop understanding of fractions as numbers." Later grades have more than one cluster devoted to fractions, but in third grade this is the only one. It is important to note that third graders do not perform operations with fractions yet; that begins in fourth grade. The emphasis in the third grade is to get to know fractions as numbers before adding, subtracting, multiplying, or dividing them.

The treatment of fractions in CCSS has received a lot of praise, including from two mathematicians at UC Berkeley, Edward Frenkel and Hung-Hsi Wu.[15] I wrote a blog post in 2015 praising the standards' emphasis on presenting fractions as numbers.[16]

WRITING WITH EVIDENCE

The writing standards in ELA have also drawn praise. Beginning in sixth grade, students are asked to write persuasive prose, with the standards breaking down composition into several important tasks: identifying claims, providing reasons and evidence for the claims, organizing the claims in a logical sequence, and presenting a conclusion that follows from the argument. This approach fits well with the reading standards' emphasis on close reading (described ahead), allowing teachers to use texts studied in class as both a writing prompt and a source of evidence in student writing.

Readers who access the sixth-grade standards will find the following:

CCSS.ELA-Literacy.W.6.1

Write arguments to support claims with clear reasons and relevant evidence.[17]

CCSS.ELA-Literacy.W.6.1.a

Introduce claim(s) and organize the reasons and evidence clearly.[18]

CCSS.ELA-Literacy.W.6.1.b

Support claim(s) with clear reasons and relevant evidence, using credible sources and demonstrating an understanding of the topic or text.[19]

CCSS.ELA-Literacy.W.6.1.c
Use words, phrases, and clauses to clarify the relationships among claim(s) and reasons.[20]

CCSS.ELA-Literacy.W.6.1.d
Establish and maintain a formal style.[21]

CCSS.ELA-Literacy.W.6.1.e
Provide a concluding statement or section that follows from the argument presented.[22]

See *http://www.corestandards.org/ELA-Literacy/W/6/#CCSS.ELA-Literacy.W.6.1*

BACKWARD MAPPING FROM ANCHORS

In developing the CCSS, the authors decided to establish college and career readiness standards at the end of the twelfth grade, called "anchors" in the ELA standards, and then map the expectations backward all the way to kindergarten. Teachers routinely do this when writing lesson plans, beginning with learning goals and then plotting the incremental steps needed to reach them. As we discussed in chapter 1, a similar strategy has long been used in building curricula from educational goals and objectives. In the 1920s, John Franklin Bobbitt recorded adult activities—at both work and in the home—and decomposed them into hundreds, sometimes thousands, of discrete tasks; Bobbitt then codified these tiny bits of learning as objectives and backward mapped them over several years of schooling.

In implementation analysis, and especially as it pertains to implementing education policy, *backward mapping* has a different meaning. It starts at the bottom of the system with the very last implementer, typically a teacher, and maps upward and backward to a policy's goals. Richard Elmore has given the best description of the process:

> It begins not with a statement of intent, but with a statement of the specific behavior at the lowest level of the implementation process that generates the need for a policy. Only after that behavior is described does the analysis presume to state an objective; the objective is first stated as a set of organizational operations and then as a set of effects,

or outcomes, that will result from these operations. Having established a relatively precise target at the lowest level of the system, the analysis backs up through the structure of implementing agencies, asking at each level two questions: What is the ability of this unit to affect the behavior that is the target of the policy? And what resources does this unit require in order to have that effect? In the final stage of analysis the analyst or policymaker describes a policy that directs resources at the organizational units likely to have the greatest effect.[23]

Elmore was concerned about gaps between the expectations of policy and the realities of implementers, taking into consideration the capacity and practical constraints of each level of the system to faithfully carry out its responsibilities in pursuing a policy's intended outcomes. The model calls for a bottom-up feasibility analysis. *Forward mapping* assumes that implementation is an engineering feat controlled by policymakers. Elmore rebuts that assumption, arguing that "by assuming that more explicit policy directives, greater attention to administrative responsibilities, and clearer statements of intended outcomes will improve implementation, forward mapping reinforces the myth that implementation is controlled from the top."

The authors of CCSS employed backward mapping to develop the standards but assumed forward mapping would serve to implement them. The standards writers' mantra—"fewer, clearer, higher"—implies that previous state standards failed because they were too numerous, often vague, and not ambitious enough. That certainly is true for many states, but it evades the questions Elmore's backward mapping stresses, assuming instead that fewer, clearer, and higher standards will fix the problem and boost learning. If implementation analysis begins at the classroom level, on the other hand, at the point where teachers interact with students, the key question is: Why did some of the kids not learn the grade-level concepts and skills that the old standards called for? A series of questions— again, all rooted at the classroom level—follow: Is it because the teacher did not cover the grade-level content? Or is it because of the way the teacher is teaching? Or the instructional materials the teacher uses? Or did the gaps in children's knowledge arise because they did not learn what they were taught in previous years? Or something else?

TEXT COMPLEXITY

The ELA standards call for students to "read and comprehend complex literary and informational texts independently and proficiently."[24] When wedded to the notion of alignment, this standard implies that students in any particular grade, including students reading well below grade level, will primarily study texts at or above grade level. The requirement relates to rigor, as stated in the introduction to the K–5 Reading Standards: "Rigor is also infused through the requirement that students read increasingly complex texts through the grades. Students advancing through the grades are expected to meet each year's grade-specific standards and retain or further develop skills and understandings mastered in preceding grades."[25] The justification for such rigor cites research showing that text complexity in college is much greater than in high school and, furthermore, that the level in high school reading textbooks has dropped significantly in recent years.[26] Greater text complexity also is proposed as an equity measure, drawing on research showing that Black and Hispanic students and those from low-income families are less likely to read challenging texts in high school than other students.

The causal inference is that the weak demands of high school texts have led to lower reading ability; however, the causal arrow may point in the opposite direction. Perhaps the unwillingness or inability of students to read demanding texts has led teachers to lower textual demands. Moreover, the assumption about learning that is embedded in the two sentences on rigor cited previously can be abbreviated to "students will learn all that is taught each year, retain all that is learned, and add a full year's worth of learning each subsequent year." That is every educator's hope, but it is an idealistic statement about human learning. Slippage does occur. Even when teachers teach a perfect lesson, some students may not learn everything, some may forget what they learned in the next day or two, and some may go home and learn even more on their own.

The standards recognize that students don't learn in lockstep with a set of grade-level expectations, even one that has been carefully mapped backward from a distal goal. The ELA standards include a statement of what the standards do *not* do: "The Standards set grade-specific standards but do not define the intervention methods or materials necessary to support students who are well below or well above grade-level expectations. No set of grade-specific standards can fully reflect the great variety in abilities, needs, learning rates, and achievement levels of students in any given classroom. However, the Standards do provide clear signposts along the way to the goal of college and career readiness for all students."[27] Signposts are useful for alerting adults that a child is falling behind grade-level expectations, but they are not helpful in addressing the needs of struggling readers.

Louisa Moats is an authority on reading acquisition. She also worked on the ELA standards, coauthoring (with Marilyn Adams) the Foundational Reading Skills section. She began questioning the standards a couple of years after their release. What does Moats think of the standards' insistence that text complexity be at or above grade level?

> This aspirational goal, while admirable, may lead to destructive consequences for the 40% who are below grade level and who are deemed "at risk" for reading failure according to predictive science (Torgesen, 2004). Of particular relevance to the community concerned with dyslexia, the standards provide no guidance and no links to research on individual variation and avoid recommending interventions for students who are functioning below grade level. The implication that these students will learn to read better if they are simply handed more complex and difficult texts, and asked to function like students who learn to read easily, is wishful—and harmful—thinking.[28]

Moats also describes the Common Core as a political document representing contending philosophical camps, not a reflection of the current science on reading and math: "The CCSS document reflects the influence of widely ranging opinions from all collaborators who submitted critiques and comments, including those of state departments of education, professional groups, university professors, advocacy groups, and publishers. Thus, the CCSS purported to be consistent with research on learning to read, write, and do math, but actually reflected current and popular ideas (and misunderstandings) about learning that were acceptable to a wide range of stakeholders in 2010. In this sense, the document represents a political (and philosophical) compromise."[29]

ESCAPE HATCHES

The standards recommend measuring text complexity using three indicators: the quality of the text, a quantitative measure of readability (formulas that generate a numerical score based on the numbers of syllables in words, sentence length, and other countable characteristics of texts), and matching students to appropriate texts. As explained in appendix A: "The use of qualitative and quantitative measures to assess text complexity is balanced in the Standards' model by the expectation that educators will employ professional judgment to match texts to particular students and tasks. Numerous considerations go into such matching. For example, harder texts may be appropriate for highly knowledgeable or skilled readers, and easier texts may be suitable as an expedient for building struggling readers' knowledge or reading skill up to the level required by the Standards."[30]

Note that "harder texts may be appropriate" and easier texts "may be suitable as an expedient for building struggling readers knowledge or reading skill." This wording provides an escape hatch. The passage serves as a brief acknowledgement of the span of reading abilities found in the typical classroom. Indeed, the Northwest Evaluation Association analyzed test scores from about sixty thousand entering kindergartners and found a four- to five-year span of reading abilities, from that of a typical three-year-old to that of a typical eight-year-old.[31] Because these students are entering school for the first time, one can eliminate the quality of standards or differences in teaching in a previous year as potential causes of the disparities. As Louisa Moats suggests, the literature on remediating reading difficulties is far more complicated than simply using an easier text as "an expedient." Determining how to adequately challenge bright young readers is equally difficult.

In the math standards, the problem of students' prior knowledge not meeting prerequisite levels is addressed like this:

> What students can learn at any particular grade level depends upon what they have learned before. Ideally then, each standard in this document might have been phrased in the form, "Students who already know . . . should next come to learn . . . ." But at present this approach is unrealistic—not least because existing education research cannot specify all such learning pathways. Of necessity therefore, grade placements

for specific topics have been made on the basis of state and international comparisons and the collective experience and collective professional judgment of educators, researchers and mathematicians.[32]

These escape hatches work for standards, not teachers. They are a direct result of mapping a twelfth-grade outcome, college and career readiness, back over thirteen grade levels of schooling. They release the standards from culpability should grade-level expectations prove inappropriate for students, whether mandating that students learn the impossible or the already learned. The burden is placed on teachers to resolve these dilemmas—to know when standards should no longer have the force of standards, when they should be relaxed or tightened. But it is not easy for teachers to exercise autonomy once standards-based curriculum materials have been purchased, assessments have been administered, and accountability systems have been bolted into place. Moreover, the whole approach of standards-based reform is predicated on the notion that too much local autonomy is why standards imposed from above are needed.

TEACH TO ONE

Under the Obama administration, the US Department of Education awarded a grant to the developers of Teach to One: Math (TtO), a "blended learning" program that combines teacher- and computer-based instruction.[33] The program also features personalization, meaning that each student's curriculum is somewhat individualized—that is, tailored to match the student's strengths and weaknesses rather than presenting the same curriculum to a whole class of pupils. The individualization is based on an assessment of baseline knowledge of approximately three hundred discrete math skills that are needed for proficiency. The program was adopted by five K–8 schools in Elizabeth, New Jersey, and evaluated by a team of researchers from Teachers College, Columbia University under the auspices of the Consortium for Policy Research in Education (CPRE). The study took place over three years, focused on sixth through eighth grades, and employed a group of sixteen non-TtO schools to serve as a comparison group. This brief description does not do justice to TtO or to the evaluation, but the study's inconclusive findings on program effects are not germane to the current discussion.[34]

The relevance to the current discussion is how Common Core and the Teach to One curriculum interacted. Schools in Elizabeth knew that students would be assessed on a New Jersey state test in the spring; therefore, they set floors and ceilings limiting how far below and above grade level the math instruction generated by the program could go. Floors were generally set at two to three years below grade level and ceilings at the grade level itself. The schools did not want students straying too far from grade-level standards, so even if precocious students were capable of acceleration into above-grade-level content, they were restricted to grade-level work. In addition, schools built into the program a focused, test-prep period of grade-level content in the weeks leading up to the state assessment. In eighth grade, New Jersey school districts had the option of testing on general eighth-grade math or algebra standards. Elizabeth chose the algebra test.

The study mentions that some students were placed in material three years below grade level even though they scored lower than that on the baseline assessment. Imagine how those students' school year unfolded. These are kids for whom math is extremely difficult. Some of them, the researchers report, were immigrants to the United States who may have never before attended school. They first received math instruction that would seem very challenging. Then, no matter how they were doing, the content would abruptly shift to even more complex, perhaps unintelligible content—algebra, in preparation for the state test.

The researchers issue a caution in terms of the comparability of treatment and control groups, but the words translate into a corollary warning about rigid grade-level standards:

> A central characteristic of TtO is that students who are missing foundational math skills are provided the time and space to experience below grade-level content. One result of this differentiation is that TtO and non-TtO students with the same initial test scores likely receive quite different mathematics content during the academic year. Because TtO students may receive content that is below grade-level, their performance on state-mandated, grade-level standardized assessments may lag behind their non-TtO peers who are being exposed to new, grade-level skills over the course of the academic year . . . In other words, mere exposure to increased levels of grade-level content—although

possibly inappropriately advanced—may provide a near-term impact on grade-level assessments. But it may not be the best approach for all students in the longer term.[35]

Basing content on grade-level standards inherently conflicts with the idea of meeting students where they currently function, the approach of TtO. Especially when faced with a high-stakes test, educators are incentivized—if not forced—to give all students grade-level work, whether students are ready for it or not and whether they already know it or not.

SHIFTING THE EMPHASIS FROM FICTION TO NONFICTION

A controversy erupted in 2012 involving the amount of nonfiction and fiction taught in classrooms.[36] A fifty-fifty balance is recommended by CCSS for grades K–5. A shift toward more reading of nonfiction is urged for later grades. The purpose of emphasizing more nonfiction is to build student knowledge about the world, a powerful predictor of reading comprehension. As Dan Willingham has pointed out, once reading tests assess reading beyond the ability to decode, they become "knowledge tests in disguise."

Willingham cites the findings of Donna R. Recht and Lauren Leslie's 1988 experiment with junior high students. Students were divided into four groups based on their reading ability (high and low) and knowledge of baseball (high and low).[37] They were given a short passage to read describing a half inning of a baseball game. After reading the account, students were asked to reenact the events in the passage with figures and verbal narration (quantity) and to sort sentences from the passage in order of importance (quality). As shown in table 4.1, low-ability readers with high knowledge of baseball outscored high-ability readers with low knowledge of baseball.[38]

In the interest of building knowledge, the ELA standards urge teachers to follow a fifty-fifty division in K–8 and seventy-thirty, favoring nonfiction, in grades 9–12. Basal texts in elementary grades are dominated by fiction, often telling the stories of people in another time or land. The classic literature taught in high schools, whether American novels or the plays of Shakespeare, also contain a healthy dose of history.

TABLE 4.1   *Quantity, quality, and errors of reenactment as a function of prior knowledge and ability*

ABILITY	TOTAL POSSIBLE	HIGH PRIOR KNOWLEDGE		LOW PRIOR KNOWLEDGE	
		MEAN	SD	MEAN	SD
High					
Quantity	40	31.4	3.9	**18.8**	7.4
Quality	24	20.7	1.8	**12.7**	4.5
Error	N/A	0.1	0.3	2.2	1.9
Low					
Quantity	40	**27.5**	5.1	13.9	5.7
Quality	24	**19.4**	2.7	10.3	4.3
Error	N/A	0.7	0.9	3.6	2.7

Source: Adapted from Donna R. Recht and Lauren Leslie, "Effect of Prior Knowledge on Good and Poor Readers' Memory of Text," *Journal of Educational Psychology* 80, no. 1 (1988): table 1.

English teachers have been trained to teach literature; they are unlikely to willingly abandon instructional units, some of which they may have spent years refining based on classroom experiences. That is especially true with great fiction that they also enjoy teaching.

Defenders of the CCSS reassure English teachers that the nonfiction/fiction distributional guidelines are for the amount of reading expected of students across *all* school subjects, not only in English classes, but that solution presents obvious implementation problems. Math, science, and history teachers are not trained to teach literature, and expecting middle and high school teachers of various disciplines to coordinate their reading assignments is unreasonable. In addition, when high school test scores are released to the public, English teachers are the ones who are held accountable for reading scores, not science teachers.

How the emphasis on nonfiction plays out in the curriculum has been left to state, district, and school administrators, along with ELA teachers, to interpret—an aspect of implementing CCSS that undermines their "commonness" from place to place. Catherine Gewertz covered the controversy for *Education Week*. Writing in 2013, she summarized what she was learning from teachers: "Teachers on the receiving end of state and district guidance . . . are coming away with a variety of interpretations. A few feel they have had no choice but to dump cherished sections of literature from their classrooms to make way for more nonfiction. Others say they haven't had to change a thing, because they've always used essays, memoirs, speeches, and such to enrich their teaching of great works of fiction and poetry." Gewertz also talked to state and local officials about the messages they were sending to teachers:

> Some of those higher-ups responded by saying that teachers who were cutting out swaths of the literary canon were probably "misunderstanding" the guidance they'd been given. But at the same time, they acknowledged that all teachers need to be incorporating nonfiction into their teaching. They said that much of the burden of nonfiction texts would be carried by teachers of science, social studies, and other subjects. But I certainly didn't hear much about intensive training being offered for teachers of all these subjects to transform their practice. Or any written guidance on that distribution of effort.[39]

Does the balance of fiction and nonfiction really matter? The CCSS documents cite no evidence that reading nonfiction is more effective in teaching critical thinking than reading fiction, nor that reading informational texts instead of fiction enhances college and career readiness by building knowledge.[40] Perhaps reading informational texts can offer background knowledge that makes all kinds of reading more accessible, but that background knowledge needs to be presented in a coherent manner over several grades.

CLOSE READING

The CCSS standards advocate "close reading" of texts. Because the meaning of any text originates in the words themselves, understanding what an author means requires students to read and reread a text for its essence. The technique serves as an antidote to the tendency of contemporary educators to link literature, especially challenging prose, to readers' interests and life experiences. That approach seeks to spark the interest of young readers by promising they can find a part of themselves in the text, perhaps even something familiar to their own life experience. Close reading turns the spotlight from readers to the text itself. Everything readers need to interpret a work's meaning can be found within the "four corners of the text."

In 2013, EngageNY published a teaching guide modeling how to teach high school students the Gettysburg Address with close reading.[41] The guide was created by Student Achievement Partners. EngageNY is a website created by the New York State Education Department to provide guidance on using CCSS in the classroom. The guide's several lessons on the Gettysburg Address take four to six days to complete.

Students are immediately thrown into the deep end of the pool. In the first lesson, students read the text of the speech cold, with no background material—nothing about Lincoln himself or the Civil War or the Battle of Gettysburg or the occasion that brought Lincoln to rural Pennsylvania to deliver a speech. The stated reason for this strategy is to get students accustomed to the idea of analyzing text on its own. Providing historical context or other preparatory information (often called *prereading activities*) puts the teacher in a hand-holding role that close reading rejects. The responsibility is on students to encounter text without assistance. The guide asserts that the recommendation promotes equity: "This close reading approach forces students to rely exclusively on the text instead of privileging background knowledge and levels the playing field for all students as they seek to comprehend Lincoln's address."

Common Core advocates, especially adherents of E. D. Hirsch's Core Knowledge, argue that the standards support the acquisition of disciplinary knowledge. It's hard to square that argument with teachers not explaining the historical context of an important speech before students read it. Moreover, it's difficult to resolve the contradiction of the standards urging more informational reading to acquire knowledge but not wanting students to put that knowledge to use when encountering a text for the first time. By characterizing knowledge as *privileging*, the guide argues that collective ignorance is preferable to individual readers bringing disparate banks of knowledge to the text, the hope being that everyone knowing nothing will "level the playing field."[42]

CONCEPTUAL UNDERSTANDING

The CCSS in mathematics define rigor along three dimensions: conceptual understanding, procedural skills and fluency, and applications.[43] These three categories have a long history in K–12 mathematics, with *problem solving* often used as a synonym for *applications*. The "Key

Shifts in Mathematics Teaching" CCSS document states that math instruction should pursue the three dimensions with "equal intensity." Research supporting the call for equal intensity, whether each should be emphasized equally throughout K–12 mathematics, is not provided.

The progressive versus traditional camps in mathematics have waged war over the appropriate balance of these three components. The best way to understand the disagreement is to examine how the antagonists view their opponents' priorities. Math reformers of a progressive stripe tend to believe that traditionalists place too much value in procedural skills and fluency. They use phrases such as *rote memory* and *drill and kill* to harken back to nineteenth-century schools that forced students to memorize long lists of mindless facts and to stand and recite them in class under the threat of the lash. The term *conceptual understanding*, on the other hand, triggers warning bells for traditionalists. They have seen math programs promoting conceptual understanding that skip important computation skills, ignore precision in calculation, and, in the worst cases, are riddled with flawed mathematics.[44]

Flash cards are a tool for learning basic facts in arithmetic. Basic facts in addition consist of sums up through $9 + 9 = 18$, historically taught in first grade as students learn addition with whole numbers. Subtraction consists of the inverse facts, $18 - 9 = 9$, typically taught in second grade. Multiplication facts are often referred to as knowing the *times tables*: $2 \times 2 = 4$, $3 \times 2 = 6$, $4 \times 2 = 8$, and so on through $9 \times 9 = 81$. They are usually taught in third grade. Division facts, the inverse of the multiplication facts, are also frequently taught in third grade. Jo Boaler is a math education professor at Stanford University and a well-known progressive math reformer. In 2012, she raised concerns about the standards' call for "fluency" with math facts: "Timed math tests have been popular in the United States for years. Unfortunately, some of the wording in the Common Core State Standards may point to an increased use of timed tests. From the 2nd grade on, the common standards give math 'fluency' as a goal. Many test writers, teachers, and administrators erroneously equate fluency with timed testing."[45]

Boaler elsewhere expanded the indictment beyond timed tests to include memorization and practice of basic facts: "Mathematics facts are important but the memorization of math facts through times table repetition, practice, and timed testing is unnecessary and damaging."[46] She instead called for number sense: "People with number sense are those who can use numbers flexibly. When asked to solve 7 x 8 someone with number sense may have memorized 56 but they would also be able to work out that 7 x 7 is 49 and then add 7 to make 56, or they may work out ten 7's and subtract two 7's (70-14). They would not have to rely on a distant memory."[47]

Boaler's beliefs about long-term memory stand in opposition to the traditionalist camp's interpretation of cognitive load theory. From their point of view, knowing from memory that 7 x 8 = 56 and working out the solution using the other methods Boaler mentions are not equivalent. Our working memory has a limited capacity—being able to recall, for example, several names of new people met at a party, but not dozens of new names. Fortunately, we don't have to relearn the names of people we already know; their names are stored in long-term memory. In mathematics, routine tasks are stored in long term memory so that they can be used in operations without being scrutinized again. That frees up working memory for learning new things that are more complex.

Kirschner, Sweller, and Clark review the evidence on inquiry and discovery methods of instruction, arguing that these methods give insufficient attention to the role played by memory in higher-level thinking. As an example, they cite experiments with expert and novice chess players, who do not differ on reproducing briefly seen, randomly placed board configurations but do differ on reproducing configurations taken from real games:

> These results suggest that expert problem solvers derive their skill by drawing on the extensive experience stored in their long-term memory and then quickly select and apply the best procedures for solving problems. The fact that these differences can be used to fully explain problem-solving skill emphasizes the importance of long-term memory to cognition. We are skillful in an area because our long-term memory contains huge amounts of information concerning the area. That information permits us to quickly recognize the characteristics of a situation and indicates to us, often unconsciously, what to do and when to do it.[48]

The point here is not to resolve the dispute between traditionalists and progressives over the proper role of memorization in math learning. It is to point out how a single word—in this case, *fluency*—can trigger a debate during the implementation of standards.

IS MEMORIZATION REQUIRED?

As noted earlier, Louisa Moats described political compromises that went into the ELA standards. The math standards include compromises as well in an effort to placate contending parties in the math wars of the 1990s. Progressives such as Jo Boaler embraced the placing of conceptual understanding, applications, and procedures on equal ground. They also valued the *mathematical practices*, processes of learning math and "habits of mind" in doing mathematics. Traditionalists embraced the requirements that students know basic facts in addition and multiplication from memory (the standards omit basic facts in subtraction or division from the requirements) and that students learn to compute with whole numbers "fluently," including using the standard algorithms.

Jason Zimba, one of the lead authors of the CCSS math standards, offered some advice to parents on Fordham Institute's website in January 2016:

> Parents can also help at home with skill building and fluency practice—things like memorizing basic math facts. When it comes to skills, practice is essential. It helps students to have someone to flash the cards or pose calculations to them. I have made flashcards that we use at home, and my kids sometimes use digital apps like *Math Drills*.
>
> If you're surprised to hear me recommending flashcards, it's likely because the Common Core has been mischaracterized as "a move away from all of that." However, according to the Common Core, students are expected to know their sums and products from memory and to be fluent with the standard algorithm for each of the four basic operations (the traditional "carry" method, in the case of addition). These expectations are unlikely to be met without extensive practice.[49]

Note the phrase *know from memory*. A few months after this advice was published, Fordham Institute ran an interview with Zimba, conducted by Amber Northern. Northern points out confusion about whether *memorize* and *know from memory* are the same, recalling her dad quizzing her on math facts as a child and pointing out that the words *memorize* and *automaticity* do not appear in the math standards (CCSS-M):

> One might assume that "know from memory" is synonymous with "memorize," but apparently not. Some math folks say that there's a big difference. Yet I'm not alone in my confusion. In our latest report, *Common Core Math in the K–8 Classroom*, for instance, one grade-five teacher said, "Common Core is not the answer. Students do not know the basics needed to function in their grade level. Multiplication tables need to be memorized." She seems to think that CCSS-M does not support memorization of multiplication facts (and who knows what she thinks of "knowing from memory"?).[50]

Zimba responded that *memorizing* is a process, whereas *know from memory* is an outcome:

> I don't think the important issue here is the word choice involved in "memorize" versus "know from memory." That difference is technical: Memorizing most naturally refers to a process (such as the one you and your dad engaged in), whereas knowing more clearly refers to an end; and ends, not processes, are the appropriate subjects for a standards statement. When the teacher in your survey says, "Multiplication tables need to be memorized," I take the teacher to be saying that students need to know the multiplication table from memory. And I agree. Some experts don't, but as we can see from the text of the standards, their view did not prevail. I don't think anybody could find the sentence on page 23 unclear. (It reads *"By the end of Grade 3, know from memory all products of two one-digit numbers."*) I do know there are people who wish that the sentence had not been included. Perhaps their discomfort interferes with their reading comprehension.[51]

CONCLUSION

The Common Core contained some landmines. Increased text complexity, close reading, and a greater emphasis on nonfiction came under fire early in implementing the ELA standards. The causal assumption that more textually rigorous texts or spending more time on close reading or shifting the balance of fiction and nonfiction would boost American students' reading achievement lacked evidence. The limitations of standards applied to students who read significantly above and below grade level are obvious to anyone spending time in classrooms. Placing the onus for student-text matching on teachers can certainly be defended, but it also contradicts the essence of any state standard, that an outside authority needs to define curricular demands. Common Core solved this problem by including rhetorical escape hatches: CCSS are standards up to the point at which they don't work; at that point, poor decisions by curriculum developers or teachers are at fault. Standards advocates often bundle all of these failings up in the phrase *poor implementation.* They excuse standards for failing; they indict local educators or publishers or test designers or someone else for standards failing.

Compromises were struck in both ELA and math. Standards writers tried to thread a needle between skills-based versus holistic, literature-based approaches in reading and progressive versus traditionalist approaches in math. The math and reading wars of the 1990s were to be avoided. We discussed Louisa Moats concerns about rigid compliance to the call for complex texts and Jason Zimba's defense of memorization and practice. Zimba's effort to explain the difference between memorization as a process and to know from memory as an end makes sense, but such fastidious word selection appears strained.

The fundamental point is that careful selection in the wording of standards is a political act, one that can become undone after standards are released and interpreted by others. Don't forget, Moats and Zimba are two Common Core authors. They were obviously surprised and dismayed at how aspects of the CCSS played out among advocates and in schools. This chapter focused on the content of the standards and the in-house debates among educators that ensued. The next chapter examines the political opposition that surfaced to fight Common Core. That resistance and rebellion included political forces well outside the boundaries of education insiders.

5

RESISTANCE
AND REBELLION

In the early years of Common Core, the public overwhelmingly supported the standards. The notion of education standards, any standards, was extremely popular. But the 2013 PDK/Gallup poll, conducted just one month shy of three years after the release of CCSS, found that 62 percent of Americans had never heard of Common Core. A third of those who had heard of CCSS admitted they did not know very much about them.[1]

Rick Hess points out that Common Core flew under the radar somewhat by design. The creators of CCSS wanted to avoid the publicity that torpedoed national standards in the 1990s. Press coverage was scant. Hess reports that a LexisNexis search of all US media outlets counted 4,500 total mentions of *Common Core* from 2009 to 2011. During that same period, the term *vouchers* drew 5,500 mentions in a single year, 2011—yet CCSS would supposedly affect the education of forty million students in states that had adopted the standards, while vouchers affected, at most, about two hundred thousand students.[2]

The mapping of standards from college and career readiness back to kindergarten raised concerns from the beginning. Early childhood educators charged that CCSS contained developmentally inappropriate standards for K–3. As early as March 2010, when the draft of CCSS for public comment was released, an advocacy organization for young children called the Alliance for Childhood issued a statement expressing "grave concerns" about the standards and calling for suspension of the development of K–3 standards.[3] In 2011, Valerie Strauss of the

Washington Post published critiques of CCSS by two scholars, Samuel J. Meisels and Joanne Yatvin. The critique by Yatvin, a former president of the National Council of Teachers of English, identified specific standards she considered inappropriate for young children, including this third-grade ELA standard: "Describe the relationship between a series of historical events, scientific ideas or concepts, or steps in technical procedures in a text, using language that pertains to time, sequence, and cause/effect." She questioned whether this was an appropriate task for an eight-year-old. Yatvin also noted that of the fifty people who participated in developing the ELA standards, only one was a current elementary teacher.[4]

Others warned that the standards had not been field tested or piloted before adoption, a routine step in earlier state efforts. Diane Ravitch, an education historian and former assistant secretary of education under the first President Bush, authors a popular blog especially favored by educators who dislike school choice and test-based reform. Ravitch had written favorably about national standards for many years. She published a blog post in July 2012, observing, "I have neither endorsed nor rejected the Common Core national standards, for one simple reason: They are being rolled out in 45 states without a field trial anywhere. How can I say that I love them or like them or hate them when I don't know how they will work when they reach the nation's classrooms?"[5] Ravitch went on to point out how CCSS departed from past practice: "I have worked on state standards in various states. When the standards are written, no one knows how they will work until teachers take them and teach them. When you get feedback from teachers, you find out what works and what doesn't work. You find out that some content or expectations are in the wrong grade level; some are too hard for that grade, and some are too easy. And some stuff just doesn't work at all, and you take it out."[6]

A social media campaign against Common Core surfaced across Facebook and Twitter, and websites such as Parents Across America (politically left of center) and Truth in American Education (politically right of center) rolled out policy briefs against CCSS. Legislation to reject or modify Common Core was introduced in a few red state legislatures—Georgia, Indiana, Arizona—but was beaten back. In November of 2012, Glenda Ritz, a schoolteacher and political novice, defeated

Tony Bennett, the incumbent state superintendent in Indiana. It was a stunning upset. Bennett was a rising star in the Republican Party and enthusiastic supporter of Common Core. Although other issues also influenced the vote, and Ritz only supported a pause in implementation of CCSS, not outright rejection, antipathy toward the standards undermined Bennett's support among Tea Party activists in his own party.[7]

Bennett's defeat foreshadowed a split between two key constituencies in the Republican Party: the Tea Party and business groups. The following spring, in March 2013, *Politico* reported that Business Roundtable and the US Chamber of Commerce were launching a media blitz on Fox News in support of the standards. Complaints about CCSS had intensified on conservative talk radio and in blog posts. Right-wing populists Glenn Beck and Michelle Malkin incessantly attacked Common Core. The Republican National Committee passed a resolution against CCSS in April 2013, with the Tea Party celebrating the vote as a triumph of the people over the establishment.[8]

RESEARCH

The research community was slow to scrutinize Common Core. The 2012 Brown Center Report on American Education, which I authored, included a study that estimated CCSS's future impact on student achievement. The debate over Common Core's content obscured a crucial question: Do standards really matter? After all, state standards had been around in one form or another for at least two decades. They varied in content, pedagogical philosophy, and the amount of learning demanded of students, as well as on a host of textual qualities: clarity, specificity, coherence of topics over grade levels, and so on. What was the empirical evidence that different standards produce different outcomes?

The study investigated three questions. As discussed in chapter 3, state standards prior to CCSS had been rated by review panels, including several from the Fordham Foundation. Were standards receiving the highest grades from the Fordham Foundation associated with larger gains on NAEP? It turns out the correlations for both the fourth and eighth grades were indistinguishable from zero, whether scores from 2003 or 2009 were used in the analysis. The change in scores from 2003 to 2009 were not associated with the change in ratings either. States with highly praised standards were no more likely to produce NAEP gains than states with weak standards.[9]

The second question looked at the difficulty of demonstrating proficiency on state tests. As also discussed in chapter 3, states varied in how high they set cut points—or minimum thresholds—for students to be considered proficient in a subject. The analysis uncovered no relationship between the level of cut points and 2005 or 2009 state NAEP scores in either the fourth or eighth grade. But in the fourth grade, the study did find positive correlations for the 2005 to 2009 change in cut points and change in NAEP scores. States that raised the bar also tended to register NAEP gains. The same relationship did not exist in the eighth grade. While intriguing, the correlation only explains about 12 percent of the variance of state fourth-grade gains, and the direction of causality is difficult to determine. Setting cut points involves both a technical question—What is the minimum point on the assessment scale reflecting a proficient student's score?—and a political one—How many students can score below proficient before the test becomes politically nonviable? Cut points are initially set by panels of experts who determine what a proficient student can do at various grade levels. Changing a cut point probably favors the political consideration, thereby biasing a correlational analysis. States with rising test scores have the latitude to raise the proficiency bar; states with declining scores, and consequently larger numbers of pupils scoring below proficient, may be pressured to lower the bar.

The final question examined sources of variation in test scores. The argument that CCSS promotes equity rests on the assumption that differences in expectations and content—existing from school to school or perhaps even classroom to classroom—exacerbate achievement differences. As a set of standards shared by more than forty states, Common Core might be expected to reduce interstate variation in achievement, but what about *intrastate* variation? The schools in every state in the union had been operating under common standards since 2003. Presumably, any impact common standards could have on reducing intrastate variation in learning would have already occurred by 2012. And yet, within-state variation in NAEP scores, as gauged by standard deviations, outstrips between-state variation by four to five times. The difference in NAEP scores between Massachusetts, a perennially high-scoring state, and

Mississippi, a perennially low-scoring state, is about twenty-five points. Within-state standard deviations range from twenty-eight to thirty-five points. Every state has a miniature Massachusetts-Mississippi disparity within its own borders. Sometimes two schools demonstrating such a dramatic contrast are geographically located only a subway ride or short drive apart—and both have been operating under the same standards for a long time.

The report concluded that CCSS would have little to no impact on student achievement. The 2012 Brown Center Report was published in February. A study with a more optimistic view was released in May.

MICHIGAN STATE UNIVERSITY STUDY

A study by William Schmidt and Richard Houang of Michigan State was publicly released with great notice at the National Press Club on May 2, 2012, an event sponsored by three organizations supporting Common Core.[10] Schmidt and Houang developed a rubric in the 1990s to compare the math standards of different nations on two dimensions, focus and coherence. Schmidt and Houang analyzed the CCSS math standards along the same lines and determined that they were similar to the standards of high-scoring nations (called the *A+ countries*) on the Trends in International Mathematics and Science Study (TIMSS). Applying this rubric to the states' math standards of 2009, Schmidt and Houang found that states with standards congruent with the Common Core, after employing some statistical controls, scored higher on the 2009 eighth-grade NAEP test in math than states with standards different from CCSS. The study was published in *Educational Researcher* later in 2012, with Schmidt and Houang concluding that it was time to end the debate over Common Core and that the CCSS in math "deserve to be seriously implemented."[11]

The harshest criticism of the study came from Ze'ev Wurman, an electrical engineer and executive from Silicon Valley who worked on the California Math Standards in the 1990s, served as an adviser in the G. W. Bush administration's US Department of Education, and voted against the adoption of CCSS by California in 2010 as a member of the state commission appointed to review the Common Core standards. Wurman published his criticism on the website of the Pioneer Institute, a think tank based in Boston that served as a home to critics of Common Core. Wurman disputed Schmidt and Houang's application of their own analytical tool, pointing out that mathematical topics were conveniently reordered in the rubric to make CCSS look similar to the standards of the A+ countries. He also noted that the relationship between standards and NAEP achievement appeared to be random in the study's initial regression analysis with all fifty states. Only after examining residuals from the regression model did Schmidt and Houang divide the states into two groups, consisting of thirty-seven wealthier states and thirteen high-poverty states. New regression analyses were conducted, which included controls for demographic characteristics and how high the cut points were for scoring proficient on state tests, generating statistically significant effects.[12]

Even if the effects detected by the study are taken at face value and interpreted optimistically, are they meaningful in a real-world sense? To answer that question, an important aspect of the Schmidt and Houang study relates to the differences of within- and between-state variation. Recall that the between-state standard deviation on NAEP is about one-fourth to one-fifth the size of the typical within-state standard deviation. The paper does not report effect sizes, only significance tests for the regression coefficients (known as p-values). In the 2014 Brown Center Report on American Education, I estimated that Schmidt and Houang's analysis finds a one standard deviation increase in their congruence index—in plain English, states making their standards much more like Common Core—associated with a NAEP gain of 2.7 points on the 2009 eighth-grade math test.[13] That is about 0.35 of the between-state standard deviation (2.7 / 7.7), a noticeable effect. Using the between-state standard deviation of NAEP is perfectly reasonable when states are the unit of analysis, but potentially misleading in gauging real-world impact. Expressed in relation to the student-level standard deviation (2.7 / 39), which increases the denominator by more than five times, a change of 2.7 points is associated with only a 0.07 standard deviation change in the NAEP score. That effect would probably go unnoticed. Moreover, considering that the 2009 state standards that Schmidt and Houang used in the analysis had been in force for five to six years, the annualized estimated effect shrinks to a miniscule amount.

NEW YORK IN TURMOIL

Common Core's advocates warned that implementing the new standards would be difficult, especially for teachers and parents. Although the authors promised during CCSS development that instructional decisions would remain under the control of teachers, once states adopted CCSS, teachers were soon asked to make "instructional shifts." Leaders also attempted to prepare parents for lower test scores, arguing that assessments aligned with CCSS would contain more difficult material and hold children to higher expectations. No state illustrated the difficulties of transitioning to Common Core quite like New York. The state made two early decisions that proved consequential. It demanded that publishers give the state complete ownership of new curriculum materials, so that they could be posted online for free use, and it scheduled new Common Core–aligned assessments for the spring of 2013.[14]

The state was already fending off complaints about its assessment. In the previous year, a controversy arose about "The Pineapple and the Hare," an absurd passage on the eighth-grade ELA test about a talking pineapple who races a hare.[15] The test item had been in circulation since at least 2006 and, like many items on state assessments, was recycled by the test vendor, Pearson, for the 2012 New York ELA exam. The item confused students and struck many parents and educators as a prime example of how bad standardized tests can get. In addition, New York had agreed to include, as part of its Race to the Top grant, scores from the state assessment in evaluating classroom teachers. Now Common Core was being rolled out. The state had revised the test for 2013, but Pearson remained the preparer. Many NY teachers were unhappy about standardized testing in general, raising concerns about the amount of time tests took from classroom instruction and the unrealistic demands they placed on special needs children and English language learners. Now the results of the state's annual assessment were to be used in a formula to decide whether teachers could keep their jobs. The 2013 test score results were shocking. In New York City, only 26 percent of students in grades 3 through 8 passed the ELA test and 30 percent passed in math.[16]

New York Commissioner of Education John King scheduled a series of town hall meetings sponsored by the state Parent Teacher Association (PTA) in the fall of 2013, with the focus on hearing from the public on

Common Core. The tour did not go well. The first meeting featured parents with multiple complaints about Common Core, including speakers condemning federal influence over schools and extolling local control. Parents also complained of too much testing and that Common Core stifled creativity and prevented teachers from doing the work that they were trained to do.[17] Teachers complained that curriculum modules promised by the state's Department of Education were not yet available on the EngageNY website, and yet the state was rushing to give the new tests. Toward the end of the second meeting, held in Poughkeepsie, King was heavily booed.[18] The remaining events were cancelled. The state PTA blamed special interest groups for disrupting the meetings, but the meetings were ultimately rescheduled for late October.[19]

Long Island was the epicenter of the New York revolt against Common Core. After the 2013 test results were released, US Secretary of Education Arne Duncan responded unartfully to critics. The *Long Island Press*, in an article describing young children throwing up and wetting their pants during the state tests, had no patience with Duncan: "Education Secretary Arne Duncan dismissed these concerns, telling a group of state school superintendents at Richmond, Va., on Nov 15: 'It's fascinating to me that some of the pushback is coming from, sort of, white suburban moms who—all of a sudden—their child isn't as brilliant as they thought they were.' To the mothers and teachers witnessing Common Core's repercussions on children and students firsthand, the demeaning comment illustrates just how disconnected government administrators are to the reality in the classroom."[20] Duncan's comment was like pouring gasoline on a fire. Parents began organizing boycotts of the assessments. Teachers began pushing their unions to take a stronger stand against testing. Tea Party members opposing Common Core from the political right now had allies from other parts of the political spectrum.

WHAT WAS HAPPENING TO NCLB?

Despite its unpopularity, No Child Left Behind remained the law of the land. After the 2012 election, in which President Obama won reelection over Mitt Romney, the US Senate continued under Democratic control and the House of Representatives under Republican control. As the latest version of ESEA, NCLB was due for reauthorization in 2007, but with each party controlling a chamber of Congress, bipartisan agreement was necessary to move legislation. The country was stuck in a deep recession, called the Great Recession by many, and Congress had battled over health care for almost all of Obama's first term. Bipartisanship was not in vogue. Reauthorization would not pass until 2015, when NCLB was replaced by the Every Student Succeeds Act (ESSA).

In 2011, nearly half of the nation's schools failed the AYP provisions of NCLB, placing them in jeopardy of sanctions.[21] That number was destined to get closer to 100 percent as the law's 2014 deadline approached. The Obama administration capitalized on the predicament by announcing a waiver program. The US Department of Education would grant states waivers from NCLB's penalties if they committed to a set of school reforms favored by the administration, a list that included college- and career-ready standards, testing to identify low-performing schools, and teacher and principal evaluation systems using, at least as part of the summative judgment, progress in student test scores. There were no surprises in the list of reforms; they were essentially a repeat of the components of Race to the Top. The surprise was the use of an unpopular federal law—one several years beyond its original expiration date—to expand federal powers.

By October 2013, forty-three state waiver applications had been approved.[22] Bundling the same three education reforms—standards, testing, and teacher evaluations—in the Obama administration's major education policies demonstrated consistency, for sure, but that impression was not free from political hazards. The three policies also came to be inextricably linked to each other, and to the Obama presidency, and that was not helpful among some constituencies. In one way or another, they all represented Common Core in the public mind. When Oklahoma later rescinded Common Core, the Department of Education temporarily revoked its waiver. When the state of Washington did not include student test scores in teacher evaluations, its waiver was also temporarily revoked. Secretary Duncan was using waivers as a means of arm-twisting states into furthering the administration's education policies. Some critics of the administration called it federal overreach, and even some allies questioned the wisdom of such forceful persuasion.[23] In 2011, Mike Petrilli had warned Duncan of a potential conservative backlash, pleading, "Walk away from this one, Mr. Secretary. Please, those of us who support the Common Core are begging you."[24] The plea went unheeded.

STATES REPEAL CCSS

In March of 2014, Governor Mike Pence signed legislation formally withdrawing the state of Indiana from Common Core.[25] The state already had a commission working on replacement standards, and the governor, a Common Core opponent, noted that new standards were planned for release in April. South Carolina followed with its repeal on May 30.[26]

Oklahoma's Republican governor, Mary Fallin, supported Common Core. Rescinding CCSS adoption proved controversial as the state's implementation timeline planned on full implementation of CCSS in only a few months, for the 2014–2015 school year. Teachers had devoted time to creating curriculum in line with the new standards. Governor Fallin reluctantly signed the repeal in June, blaming federal overreach for poisoning the political landscape for common standards.[27] Reporting on the legislation for the *Washington Post*, Lindsey Layton observed, "In Oklahoma, where all 77 counties voted against Obama in 2012, any hint of support from the Obama administration was enough to energize opposition."[28]

Missouri, North Carolina, and Utah all passed mandatory reviews of the CCSS. In addition to red state, anti-Obama sentiments and the activism of the Tea Party, another influence on anti–Common Core legislation was lingering resentment about how Common Core originated, starting with that first planning meeting in Chicago. In most states, the governor, with the state board or state superintendent, approved the CCSS without legislative action. State legislatures were reasserting their power. "Legislators were just totally left out of it when the states first adopted the Common Core, and that was a mistake," said Kathy Christie of the Education Commission of the States, a nonpartisan organization that monitors state education policy. "And this is the reaction."[29]

PARTISAN DIVIDE

Ed Next has conducted a series of polls on Common Core. The surveys trace a dramatic decline in Common Core support from 2013 through

2017 (see table 5.1). To measure whether the brand name *Common Core* was affecting responses from people who otherwise supported common standards across states, random samples of respondents were asked two questions that were identical except for the use of the words *Common Core*. In the question identifying Common Core by name, supporters of CCSS swamped opponents by five to one among the 2013 poll respondents, 64 percent to 13 percent. Only three years later, in 2016, the two sides were dead even at 42 percent to 42 percent. Subsequent polls in 2017 and 2018 showed the slide in support for CCSS stabilizing in the mid- to low 40 percent area (41 percent in 2017 and 45 percent in 2018), then rising to 50 percent in 2019.

Table 5.2 displays support for Common Core among Democrats, Republicans, and teachers. Several patterns are interesting. The Common Core label depressed support for common standards among all three groups in 2014, and it continued to do so in 2019. The rebound in public support for Common Core from 2017 to 2019 appears to be primarily due to strengthening support among Republicans (from 32 percent to 46 percent with Common Core named). Despite the rebound, teachers and Republicans remained the least supportive of Common Core in 2019. Only 44 percent of teachers and 46 percent of Republicans supported Common Core when named.

The partisan divide on Common Core can also be seen in the assessments that states used in 2019. In 2010, the two Common Core

TABLE 5.1   *Education Next polls on standards, with and without Common Core name, 2013 to 2019*

PROMPT	POSITION	2013	2014	2015	2016	2017	2018	2019
With name	Support	64	53	49	42	41	45	50
	Oppose	13	26	35	42	38	38	40
Without name	Support	–	68	54	55	61	61	66
	Oppose	–	17	30	28	20	26	25

Source: Michael B. Henderson et al., "Public Support Grows for Higher Teacher Pay and Expanded School Choice," *Education Next*, last updated August 20, 2019, https://www.educationnext.org /school-choice-trump-era-results-2019-education-next-poll/#commoncore.

Note: The question with the name omitted was not asked in 2013.

TABLE 5.2   *Education Next polls on standards; Democratic, Republican, and teacher support with and without Common Core named, 2013 to 2019*

GROUP	NAME?	2013	2014	2015	2016	2017	2018	2019
Democrats	With	67	63	57	49	49	52	52
	Without	–	69	58	58	61	64	66
Republicans	With	64	43	37	35	32	38	46
	Without	–	68	50	53	64	58	67
Teachers	With	76	46	40	41	45	43	44
	Without	–	53	48	46	46	48	51

Source: Michael B. Henderson, David Houston, Paul E. Peterson, Martin R. West, "Public Support Grows for Higher Teacher Pay and Expanded School Choice," *Education Next*, last updated August 20, 2019, https://www.educationnext.org/school-choice-trump-era-results-2019-education-next-poll/#commoncore.

Note: The question with the name omitted was not asked in 2013.

assessment consortia, Smarter Balanced Assessment Consortium and PARCC, comprised forty-six states, but states steadily dropped out from 2010 to 2020. In table 5.3, states are classified as Democratic or Republican based on one party having full control of the state legislature and governor's office. States with mixed control are classified as such. Nebraska has a bicameral legislature elected without party affiliation and a Republican governor. It is coded Republican.

Democratic states overwhelmingly administered the Common Core–based tests (eleven to four), either PARCC or Smarter Balanced; the Republican states decidedly did not use them (two to twenty); and mixed states fell in the middle (five to eight). The only Republican states using PARCC or Smarter Balanced were Idaho and South Dakota. Idaho's legislature was seriously considering legislation to repeal its Common Core standards in 2020.[30] South Dakota revised its standards in 2018, and although state superintendent Don Kierkegard declared that "Common Core standards are officially gone," the new standards look a lot like the old ones.[31] As of 2020, the state still participated in Smarter Balanced.

The only Democratic states not using PARCC or Smarter Balanced in 2019 were New York, Rhode Island, Maine, and Virginia. Each has a story. New York's early political troubles with Common Core persuaded the state to revise its standards and assessment. Rhode Island decided to

TABLE 5.3   *State political party dominance and choice of assessment in 2019*

PARTY DOMINANCE	PARCC OR SBAC	OTHER TEST
Democratic	11 (73%)	4 (27%)
Mixed	5 (38%)	8 (62%)
Republican	2 (9%)	20 (91%)
Total	**18**	**32**

Source: National Conference of State Legislatures. Data current as of December 1, 2019. Assessments of the Partnership for Assessment of Readiness for College and Career (PARCC) and Smarter Balanced Assessment Consortium (SBAC) are aligned with the CCSS.

Note: Colorado, Louisiana, and Michigan use a mix of PARCC or SBAC items with their own test and are counted as SBAC/PARCC states. State tests in use taken from Catherine Gewertz, "Which States Are Using PARCC or Smarter Balanced?," *Education Week*, February 15, 2017, last updated April 9, 2019, https://www.edweek.org/ew/section/multimedia/states-using-parcc-or-smarter -balanced.html.

use the highly regarded MCAS assessment of its neighboring state, Massachusetts. Maine adopted Common Core but joined neither CCSS assessment consortium, experimenting instead with a "proficiency-based" assessment system.[32] Virginia never adopted Common Core; it was a red state in 2010 and only turned blue in the 2019 election. It continued to use the Standards of Learning, which include tests in science and history/social science, as the state assessment.

In addition to partisanship, the Common Core–based tests encountered technical challenges as they were introduced into schools.[33] Both Smarter Balanced and PARCC are online assessments. Montana's first run at Smarter Balanced in 2015 experienced so many system crashes and technical glitches that only 72 percent of its tests were deemed usable. Tennessee's system froze from too many users coming online at once, then broke down, and the state refused to pay its vendor. Wisconsin and North Dakota had similar problems. Nevada was a complete disaster, with only 37 percent of the 2015 tests completed.[34] Technical problems are not unique to Common Core assessments, of course—they can happen to any assessment offered online for the first time—but the Common Core tests did involve an extra layer of management that complicated matters. The states hired vendors to administer the tests, who then received source codes from the test consortia. Smarter Balanced, for example, had five different vendors, all competing against each other, scattered across eighteen states.[35]

OPT-OUT MOVEMENT

The rebellion that began in New York in 2013 spread beyond the state and matured into a full-fledged opt-out movement, encouraging parents to boycott state tests. In 2015, Karen McGee, head of the New York State United Teachers, endorsed opting out of state tests. The opt-out movement was fueled by political opposition to standardized testing in general—and not specifically against Common Core—but it gathered steam in 2015 as tests associated with Common Core were being administered in many states for the first time. Stories that teachers were being evaluated based on test results in subjects they did not even teach increased the sense that testing was both unfair and out of control.[36] The New Jersey Education Association ran television ads attacking PARCC for six weeks during the spring assessment season.[37]

In 2016, twelve states were warned by the US Department of Education that they fell below the 95 percent participation rate in state assessments mandated by law. Under ESSA, states had to file a plan for how to deal with schools falling below that threshold.[38] In 2015 and 2016, eighty-seven opt-out bills were filed in state legislatures. Bills made it into law in five states (Colorado, Georgia, Oregon, Utah, and Wisconsin), protecting the rights of parents to remove children from state tests and standardizing procedures for adjudicating parental requests.[39]

Data from New York and Colorado suggested that parents opting out tended to be suburban, white, and middle- to upper-middle class.[40] Opt-out rates were much higher in Long Island and upstate New York districts than in New York City. The movement appeared to peak during the 2015 and 2016 tests, but it did continue to affect test-taking rates, especially in New York. In 2019, nearly half of grade 3 through 8 children in Long Island school districts opted out of the NY state ELA assessment.[41]

SOCIAL MEDIA OPPOSITION

Angry parents were not the only group complaining about Common Core on social media. The internet also included an organized political effort to undermine the standards. Jonathan Supovitz and colleagues at the Consortium for Policy Research in Education analyzed almost one million tweets about Common Core posted on Twitter from September 2013 through April 2016. They found that opponents' tweets fell into five frames: (1) government controlling children's lives through CCSS; (2) use of CCSS for corporate profit; (3) CCSS as an enemy in the culture wars; (4) CCSS as an experiment on children; and (5) CCSS as a way to brainwash children.[42] The first, third, and fifth frames appeal to the political right. The second frame appeals to the political left. The fourth frame appeals to opponents on both sides of the political spectrum. Although about 190,000 individuals sent tweets opposing Common Core, a far-right bot run out of Florida, the Patriot Journalist Network, accounted for about one-fourth of all tweets during the final year of the study. It was able to "borrow" followers' Twitter accounts and send out masked tweets that looked as if they were coming from individuals.[43]

THE 2016 CAMPAIGN FOR PRESIDENT

By the end of 2015, defenders of Common Core were in retreat. Governor Cuomo of New York announced that implementation of standards had failed, and he appointed a commission to study the standards and recommend a new course for the state. US Secretary of Education Arne Duncan declared a moratorium on the use of test results in teacher evaluation systems supported by Race to the Top grants.[44] As mentioned earlier, the Every Student Succeeds Act, successor to NCLB, was signed into law, sharply restricting the federal government's ability to ever again attempt to influence state-adopted standards, assessments, or teacher evaluations. Randi Weingarten, president of the American Federation of Teachers, told Lindsey Layton of the *Washington Post*, "I've never seen both Democrats and Republicans want to curb the authority of the federal Department of Education the way they want to now."[45]

The 2016 presidential campaign for the Republican nomination featured a newcomer to politics, Donald J. Trump, who immediately became a Tea Party favorite. Trump blasted former or sitting governors Chris Christie of New Jersey, Scott Walker of Wisconsin, and Bobby Jindal of Louisiana for originally supporting Common Core and then turning against the standards once support collapsed. Jeb

Bush of Florida continued to support Common Core, but he remained on the defensive and softened his enthusiasm for Common Core under Trump's attacks.[46]

MATH ITEMS GO VIRAL

The comedian Louis C. K. appeared on *Late Night with David Letterman* on May 1, 2014.[47] He had been helping his two daughters with their homework and spent several days on Twitter railing against their Common Core math curriculum. When he appeared on Letterman's show, Louis C. K. said his kids had been preparing for the state's standardized tests. When Letterman asked what the consequences were for the testing, Louis C. K. cracked, "The way I understand it, if the kids don't do well, they burn the school down." He then described the "new way" of thinking about math: "Bill has three goldfish. He buys two more. How many dogs live in London?"

The joke got a big laugh. It touched a nerve about the head-scratching math problems parents were seeing under the label *Common Core*. Many of the problems coming home even included in the margin the specific Common Core learning objective that the item was intended to meet. Some of these items became famous overnight as Facebook and Pinterest pages popped up on which frustrated parents shared the latest outrage.

Allow me to describe a few of the math problems that were widely circulated. Unfortunately, copyright obstacles prevent us from showing the items themselves. I will do my best to describe them, but readers are urged to visit the URLs provided in the endnotes and examine the items. The selected problems are not meant to represent Common Core mathematics. Some of them predate Common Core and were recycled by publishers. They aren't even meant to represent items that irritated parents. They are meant to give the flavor of the social media on Common Core. They all illustrate aspects of Common Core's emphasis on conceptual understanding of mathematics.

The first item asks students, "Tell how to make 10 when adding 8 + 5."[48] The student's answer, in a first-grader's scrawl, is: "You cannot make 10 with 8 + 5." The teacher responds in a blue marker, "Yes you can. Take 2 from 5 and add it to 8 (8 + 2 = 10), then add 3."

The item refers to a strategy for mental addition called *making 10s* that has been taught to first and second graders for years. This student knows that 8 + 5 does not equal 10. The sum, 8 + 5 = 13, is a math fact traditionally memorized in first grade, along with all single-digit sums up to 9 + 9 = 18. The item is really designed to see whether students know the make 10 strategy. A student who knows by heart that 8 + 5 = 13 would be dumbfounded as to why one would use a two-step technique (8 + 2 = 10, and then 3 more equals 13) to solve such a simple problem. The teacher's explanation does not help the mismatch of the item's intention and the student's interpretation of what is being asked.

Another item that circulated on social media appears to be not a problem, but an explanation from a textbook or worksheet.[49] It also involves the making 10s strategy, this time applying it to adding two two-digit numbers: 26 + 17 = ?. The explanation is convoluted:

Add 26 + 17 by breaking apart numbers to make a ten.

Use a number that adds with the 6 in 26 to make a 10.

Since 6 + 4 = 10, use 4.

Think: 17 = 4 + 13.

Add 26 + 4 = 30.

Add 30 + 13 = 43.

So, 26 + 17 = 43.

This explanation has too many steps for a first grader to follow. I could imagine a teacher demonstrating the solution visually with a marker on a number line, showing that 26 + 17 can be solved by starting at 26, then adding 4 (moving the marker to 30), then adding 13 (moving the marker to 43). The final move is 13 units because 13 is the amount "left over" from 17 after moving 4 units. The item's explanation is correct but confusing as worded. I am assuming this example served as an introduction to several practice problems, and it's no wonder why many students did not know what to do.

The most famous Common Core math item is often called Jack's Problem.[50] It went viral after a frustrated father posted the item on Facebook and then went on television to share his response. The item shows the subtraction problem 427 − 316 being solved by a fictional student named Jack, who gets a wrong answer, 121. Students are asked to write a letter to Jack telling him what he did right and how he can fix his mistake.

A visual is provided showing Jack's work. Jack uses a strategy known as *skip counting*. Jack's task is to skip count 316 units backward from 427. A number line is shown with Jack skip counting backwards in several steps: first three times in increments of 100 (thereby subtracting a total of 300 and landing on 127 on the number line), then subtracting 6 more single units, arriving at the incorrect answer, 121. Jack's error is that he forgot to subtract the 10 in 16. Had he done so, he would have arrived at the correct answer, 111.

Here's the letter to Jack that the frustrated father wrote:

Dear Jack,

Don't feel bad. I have a bachelor of science degree in electronics engineering which included extensive study in differential equations and other higher math applications. Even I cannot explain the Common Core mathematics approach, nor get the answer correct. In the real world, simplification is valued over complication.

Therefore,

$$\begin{array}{r} 427 \\ -\ 316 \\ \hline 111 \end{array}$$

The answer is solved in under 5 seconds—111.

The process used is ridiculous and would result in termination if used.

This is a bad problem. It was given to a second grader. It's far too difficult for someone just beginning to learn subtraction. Attempting to diagnose what another person is doing wrong mathematically and explaining how to fix the error is a sophisticated—and valuable—task, but a problem of this type is appropriate for an adult in a teacher-training program, not a second grader. And the amount of writing needed to answer the question adequately is far beyond what a second grader can do.

Much of the father's confusion is caused by the number line being drawn wrong, with the distance from 121 to 127 (6 units) somehow larger than any of the three jumps of 100 units. The father saw the counting backward by hundreds (three times) to get from 427 to 127, but, thinking that this was a properly scaled number line, he then started counting by tens and made a complete mess of the problem. He then shows how easily the problem is solved using the standard algorithm for subtraction.

The Common Core math authors denounced the item. Interviewed by the *Hechinger Report*, Jason Zimba said flatly, "That question would not be in a textbook if I wrote it." William McCallum pointed out that CCSS does not call for this method of subtraction but does call for fluency with the standard algorithm. "Complaining that this is a Common Core method when the Common Core doesn't require this method, but does require the method he wants, it's just a lie," McCallum said, commenting on the frustrated father.[51]

McCallum is right. Common Core requires that students can fluently use the standard algorithm in subtraction. He's also right that Common Core does not *require* this method of subtraction. But the Common Core does encourage using number lines to solve problems, counting by tens and hundreds to do mental arithmetic (as illustrated with the making 10s example), employing models to show place value, evaluating other students' mathematics, and communicating mathematical reasoning in writing. This a bad math problem, but its publisher was trying to be consistent with those recommendations.

Zimba and McCallum made another, very important point in the *Hechinger Report* article. Common Core is a set of standards, not a curriculum. Others develop curriculum materials. Some will be good and some will be bad. And some of the bad materials might be very bad.

Fortunately, kids have a way of steering around tasks that they view as absurd. An often-heard complaint about Common Core is the amount of writing students are asked to do in mathematics, especially when explanations are required for simple answers. Two of the cleverest explanations that circulated widely on social media were also cute relief from Common Core's frequently acrimonious debate.

Here's the first one:

Mike saw 17 blue cars and 25 green cars at the toy store.
How many cars did he see?

Write a number sentence with a box for the missing number. Explain
how the number sentence shows the problem.[52]

This second grader wasn't going to mess around with an empty box,
instead writing the number sentence, 17 + 25 = 42, and then drawing a
box around the 42. The second grader's wee bit ungrammatical explanation: "I got the answer by talking in my brain and I agreed of the answer
that my brain got."

A first grader was equally adept at fending off ridiculousness.[53] The
problem was this:

Bobby had four dimes.

Amy has 30 pennies.

Which child has more money?

The student answered "Bobby," the correct answer. Then the student was
asked: How do you know? Show your thinking. The student drew a stick
figure self-portrait, hand positioned reflectively on forehead. Thought
bubbles rose up to a cloud containing: "Bobby."

Now, that's how to show your thinking.

CONCLUSION

The opt-out movement succeeded in drawing attention to standardized
tests and casting them in a bad light. By emphasizing the amount of
time devoted to test prep, the narrowing of curriculum to math and
ELA, the unfairness of evaluating teachers based on test scores, and the
foibles of computerized assessment, critics of standardized testing created doubts about assessments just as the Common Core–based tests,
PARCC and Smarter Balanced, were being rolled out in schools. The
impact was felt particularly in New York. In the fall of 2015, Governor
Cuomo announced a task force that would review the state's standards
and assessments.[54]

The pushback on standardized testing was part of a larger political
dynamic, of a public largely unaware of CCSS and shut out of the standards' development until teaching materials and assessments arrived in
classrooms. The opposition was bipartisan—but only to a point. Teachers'

union members and Tea Party activists worked hard to defeat the implementation of Common Core, but their opposition was, in Patrick McGuinn and Jonathan Supovitz's words, more "in parallel" than a true bipartisan coalition. McGuinn and Supovitz use the term *transpartisan* to describe the coalition: "The early phase of the Common Core Standards movement was notable for its carefully crafted bipartisan approach. The developers of the standards and their advocates took great pains to create broad support and to avoid the stigma of federal control by working through the CCSSO and NGA to brand the standards as state-led. The economic recession, the federal stimulus package, and the opportunistic way in which the RTTT incented rapid standards adoption, however, undid much of the groundwork paved by the decentralized strategy of the common standards."[55]

This analysis seems on the mark except for overstating the bipartisan nature of Common Core's development. It applies to Washington-based elites. For those who wanted something akin to national standards and saw a federal effort as politically dangerous, a compromise was indeed reached by "working through CCSSO and NGA to brand the standards as state-led." That allowed the developers to say these were state standards and not federal. For teachers and parents, of course, the distinction between federal and state—or between state and district for that matter—is irrelevant if an outside authority is imposing an ill-fitting regime on your school.

For other groups, rather than agreeing to a lasting compromise, Common Core advocates each singled out an element in the standards that they had either long advocated or believed could be achieved during implementation. Accountability hawks and teachers' unions did not think for a minute about compromising on holding local educators responsible for student learning, nor did traditionalists and progressives consider compromising on the curricular content of ELA or math. Their political support of CCSS was contingent on their ideas surviving the unknown tribulations of standards being enacted in schools. The Common Core advocates who were more interested in the standards' content than their federal or state origins could find something they liked in the standards, and they imagined that the fruits of their favorite parts of Common Core would be harvested after implementation. Sometimes they were disappointed. This point will be taken up again in chapter 7, which examines how Common Core affected curriculum and instruction.

The impact of social media on Common Core's politics is unmistakable, but it is too easy to conflate tales of parent frustration and ridicule of incomprehensible homework assignments with the organized ideological opposition clearly evident on Twitter. The resistance that Common Core experienced in the early days of implementation misled some of its backers into thinking that the opposition could be addressed through better messaging.[56] State legislatures that subsequently passed laws mandating revisions to the standards, withdrawal from the two assessment consortia, or the recognition of parents' rights to opt out of state tests signaled that Common Core's political challenges were not just a public relations problem.

6

EFFECTS ON STUDENT ACHIEVEMENT

Public policies must be carefully studied to determine their impact. Several aspects of Common Core make it difficult to evaluate whether the policy is a success or failure. A typical approach is for analysts to compare outcomes of governmental units (in this case, states) that adopt a policy to those that do not. Analysts sort states into a treatment group, those adopting the policy, and a control or comparison group, the states not adopting the policy. States—and the districts and schools within them—are constantly adopting new policies and modifying or abandoning old policies. How can Common Core, or any other policy, be singled out as causing student achievement to rise or fall? Maybe it was one of the other policies or a mix of policies that produced the effect. Perhaps it was a factor outside the education system—for example, a sudden downturn or pickup in the economy or a drastic change in the general well-being of children.

Advocates have a habit of claiming that their favorite policy produced a beneficial effect when a single state's test scores rise after a policy's adoption. Critics do the opposite, blaming policies they don't like for a state's test score decline. The worst case of this happens when a governor or mayor takes credit for rising test scores or when a political opponent blames an incumbent when scores fall. No serious analyst believes such claims have a legitimate causal basis.

Techniques do exist to isolate causal effects. Joshua D. Angrist and Jorn-Steffen Pishke present a noneducation example, examining how reducing the legal age for drinking alcohol affects teen suicides and death from auto accidents.[1] After the end of Prohibition, most states set a minimum age of twenty-one to purchase alcohol, but some, including New York and Louisiana, set eighteen years of age as the threshold. In 1971, the twenty-sixth amendment lowered the national voting age to eighteen. Responding to the argument that citizens who are old enough to vote or to fight in Vietnam should be allowed to buy beer, states began lowering the drinking age. Comparing teen traffic fatalities in states that previously had a twenty-one-year-old minimum and then lowered it to states already allowing younger drinkers is an intuitively appealing analytical approach, especially if potential confounding influences are taken into account. Angrist and Pishke employ a *differences in differences* strategy, comparing changes in treatment and comparison groups. Each state can then serve as its own control for unobserved influences on traffic deaths. Unobserved influences are factors on which analysts do not have data—for example, cultural values that may lead teens to drink more or drive recklessly in some states compared to others—but which may confound the analysis. The differences in differences analytical strategy assumes that unobserved confounders are "baked into the cake" at baseline, remain stable over the treatment period, and are therefore subtracted out in the calculation of trends.[2]

What about Common Core? Forty-six states initially adopted Common Core in English language arts, leaving only four states (Alaska, Nebraska, Texas, and Virginia) to serve as a comparison group. Minnesota did not adopt the Common Core mathematics standards, so the comparison group increases its membership to five states in that case, but five is still a small group. Large changes for any one state in a small group—test scores sharply moving up or down—can dramatically influence the average outcome of the whole group.

CENTER FOR STANDARDS, ALIGNMENT, INSTRUCTION, AND LEARNING STUDY (SONG, YANG, AND GARET)

The Center for Standards, Alignment, Instruction, and Learning (C-SAIL) is housed at the University of Pennsylvania and funded by a grant from the Institute for Education Sciences. In 2019, C-SAIL released a study examining the effects of college and career readiness (CCR) standards on state NAEP scores. The study was conducted by three researchers from the American Institutes for Research—Mengli Song, Rui Yang, and Michael Garet—and released in a monograph titled *Effects of State's Implementation of College- and Career-Ready Standards on Student Achievement.*[3] The use of the phrase *college and career readiness standards* rather than *Common Core* follows C-SAIL's stated mission to investigate education standards writ large, of which Common Core is only one example. Indeed, the center has published in-depth studies of college and career readiness standards in a few states, including Texas, a noted nonadopter of Common Core. Despite that qualification, the study was received by education media as an evaluation of Common Core. Indeed, shortly after its release, Mengli Song published an article explaining the main findings, with the title posing the question, "Did Common Core Standards Work?"[4]

Study's Design

The C-SAIL study employs a comparative interrupted time series design using state NAEP scores. In education, interrupted time series analyses typically examine test scores before and after a treatment, with the date of a policy intervention pinpointing the interruption—the point in time demarcating the two periods. The technique is a form of the differences approach Angrist and Pishke used to assess the effects of a lower legal age to buy alcohol. Incorporating a comparison group involves calculating the trends of both treatment and comparison groups and seeing whether the changes in the two groups' trend lines differ before and after the intervention.

The C-SAIL researchers used two ratings of state standards in place before Common Core to assign states to treatment and comparison groups. The 2010 ratings of the Fordham Institute were used to create a *prior rigor index* (PRI) for both ELA and math standards. The Fordham Institute rated states on a scale from 0 to 7, with 7 indicating the most rigorous standards and 0 indicating the least rigorous. The C-SAIL study designates states with 0 to 3 ratings as *treatment states* and 5 to 7 as *comparison states*. States with a 4 rating were excluded to provide a sharper contrast.

The logic of the rules for group assignment is that states with less rigorous standards in 2010 would experience the most change after adopting Common Core. States with rigorous standards already in place in 2010 would experience the least change because they already held high expectations for students. The point of interruption is set as 2010 because that is when most states formally adopted college- and career-ready standards. States adopting the new standards in any year other than 2010 were excluded. NAEP scores prior to 2010, going back to 1990, serve to estimate the pre-CCSS trend.

The second rating system, called the *prior similarity index* (PSI), is based on a 2009 rating system by Michigan State University (MSU) researchers that evaluated whether state math standards in existence in 2009 were similar to Common Core's math standards. The MSU study created a five-point scale. In the C-SAIL analysis, states with standards coded as 1s and 2s were deemed the least similar and 4s and 5s the most similar to Common Core. States with 3s were excluded to provide a sharper contrast. The PSI is only available for math; the MSU researchers did not evaluate standards in ELA or reading. The logic of the sorting rule is the same as for the PRI: states with math standards similar to CCSS experienced a less demanding change than states with math standards similar to CCSS.

For this discussion, Washington, DC, is considered a "state," leading to fifty-one state NAEP scores. The sorting rules created the following groups:

> Twenty treatment and fourteen comparison states using the PRI for math, with seventeen states excluded.

> Seventeen treatment and twelve comparison states using the PRI for reading, with twenty-two states excluded.

> Fourteen treatment and twelve comparison states for the PSI for math, with twenty-five states excluded.

Results of the Study

In the PRI analysis, the C-SAIL study discovered negative effects of CCRs on achievement, with the effects on fourth-grade reading and eighth-grade math reaching statistical significance. The PSI analysis uncovered no significant effects. Bear in mind that statistical significance is not the same thing as real-world significance. The negative effects indicated by the PRI are quite modest in terms of substantive magnitude, about one-tenth of a standard deviation.

Let's focus our attention on the PRI analysis. Table 6.1 displays the findings.

Notice that the negative effect is a little less than four NAEP points in both fourth-grade reading (–3.8) and eighth-grade math (–3.9). A one-tenth of a standard deviation difference in test scores is usually considered difficult to detect by the naked eye, and especially so if it represents the cumulative impact of several years of policy effort. The most striking finding of the study was that the negative effects of CCR standards appear to increase over time. Figure 6.1 examines fourth-grade reading, comparing the NAEP scores predicted for the treatment group in the post-CCR period to the actual scores registered by those states. The graph illustrates the comparison of "what would have happened without CCR standards" (the dashed line) to what actually happened (the solid line). After the adoption of CCR standards in 2010 (the vertical line), the two lines steadily diverge, with the largest differences registered in 2017. That divergence is even more evident for eighth-grade math scores (see figure 6.2). The C-SAIL study pours cold water on the hope that implementation, although slow, will eventually produce positive outcomes.

Strengths and Weaknesses of the Study

The C-SAIL study possesses many strengths. The study is the first technically sophisticated evaluation of Common Core after the standards' near decade of existence. An interrupted time series is a widely accepted

TABLE 6.1   *Estimated effects of CCR standards on NAEP scores, 2010–2017, using the prior rigor index*

	READING FOURTH	MATH FOURTH	READING EIGHTH	MATH EIGHTH
NAEP scale core/(SD)	–3.8* (1.9)	–2.2 (1.8)	–2.1 (1.7)	–3.9* (2.0)
SD Units (based on 2017 SD)	–0.10	–0.07	–0.06	–0.10

Source: Mengli Song, Rui Yang, and Michael Garet, *Effects of States' Adoption of College- and Career-Ready Standards on Student Achievement*, data from table 3.

*p < 0.05.

FIGURE 6.1   *Observed average NAEP grade 4 reading scores for treatment states identified based on the prior rigor index and their predicted scores in the absence of CCR standards*

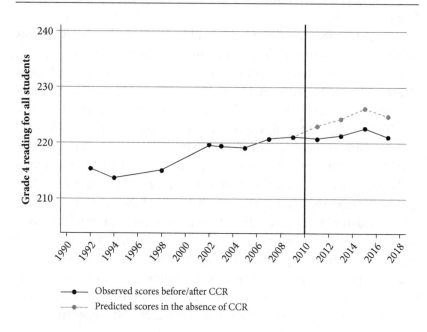

Observed scores before/after CCR
Predicted scores in the absence of CCR

Source: Mengli Song, Rui Yang, and Michael Garet, *Effects of States' Adoption of College- and Career-Ready Standards on Student Achievement*, figure 1. Reprinted with permission of authors.

quasi-experimental technique. States are the unit of analysis; however, the authors choose not to express effects in the standard deviation of the regression coefficient, which, as explained in chapter 5, reflects between-state variation. The authors instead express effects in relation to NAEP's student-level standard deviation. This produces a more realistic estimate. The study includes an extensive set of state-level covariates in its analysis, some policy related and some not, including per pupil spending, student demographic characteristics, and pupil-teacher ratios. The study enters these covariates as time variant in the statistical analyses, meaning simply that the states' status on the covariates are entered for multiple years and allowed to change from entry to entry.

There are also weaknesses. The authors state that the C-SAIL study's analytical approach was influenced by two studies of No Child Left Be-

FIGURE 6.2   *Observed average NAEP grade 8 math scores for treatment states identified based on the prior rigor index and their predicted scores in the absence of CCR standards*

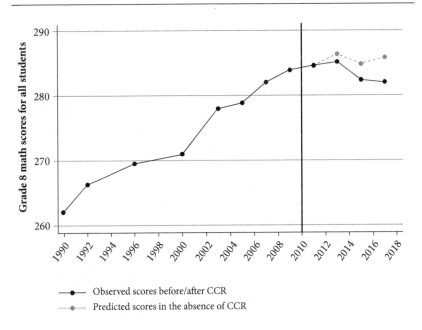

            ●── Observed scores before/after CCR
            ●── Predicted scores in the absence of CCR

Source: Mengli Song, Rui Yang, and Michael Garet, *Effects of States' Adoption of College- and Career-Ready Standards on Student Achievement*, figure C.3. Reprinted with permission of authors.

hind, the first conducted by Thomas Dee and Brian Jacob and the second by Manyee Wong and colleagues, both discussed in chapter 3.[5] Recall that these earlier studies found that the test-based state accountability systems required by NCLB produced positive effects on NAEP scores in mathematics, especially in the fourth grade, but had weak to no effect on reading scores. Interestingly, the C-SAIL study includes controls for some education policies but does not include a variable for accountability policies, which is odd considering that the two earlier studies found accountability influential. The consequences of the omission may be amplified in the post-CCSS period considering that other C-SAIL researchers have discovered that states moved toward softer forms of accountability, systems that are "supportive, not punitive."[6] If accountability matters and some states have fundamentally changed their approach, it seems important to control for accountability policies in an analysis with policy covariates.

The C-SAIL procedure for assigning states to treatment or comparison groups leads to some counterintuitive sorting of states. The states that explicitly rejected the Common Core math standards (Alaska, Minnesota, Nebraska, Texas, and Virginia) are omitted from most of the study's analyses, having adopted their alternative standards in a year other than 2010.[7] The purpose of a comparison group is to estimate the counterfactual—in this case, to predict what would have happened if Common Core had not been adopted. Excluding the states that in fact did not adopt Common Core seems incongruous to that objective. Their omission makes the study similar to a study of dosage. All of the states in the study adopted Common Core (or college- and career-ready standards), but it was more of a stretch, a bigger change in standards, for the treatment states than for the comparison states.

As mentioned, the covariates in the analysis are time variant; they change to reflect data current to each NAEP year. The calculation of the pre-CCR trend includes NAEP scores dating back to the first main NAEP assessment in 1990.[8] But the study does not model the main variable of interest, standards, as time variant in either the pre- or post-CCR periods. For its 2010 review, the Fordham Institute evaluated each state's 2009 standards. In effect, the quality of each state's 2009 standards is locked in as a static representation of standards for the entire pre-CCSS period. The fact is that many states changed their standards—some more than once—between 1992 and 2009.

The Fordham Institute's 2010 review was not its first. Reviews were also conducted in 1998 (ELA and math), 2000 (several subjects), and 2005 (math). Using those reviews to model the quality of pre-CCSS standards would have led to different state groupings. The Fordham Institute did not rate the states on content and rigor in 2005 (the C-SAIL criteria), but it did give letter grades on an A to F scale to indicate overall quality.

Let's take a look at the Fordham Institute's 2005 and 2010 ratings and examine some of the differences. Table 6.2 displays states that adopted CCSS and have discrepancies of at least two grade levels in the Fordham Institute's evaluations of 2005 and 2010. C-SAIL researchers would have almost certainly categorized these states differently had 2005 ratings instead of 2010 ratings been used as sorting criteria.

TABLE 6.2   *State standards with letter-grade changes of at least two levels: Thomas B. Fordham Institute, 2005 and 2010*

ELA		
STATE	2005	2010
Delaware	C	F
District of Columbia	C	A
Illinois	B	D
Mississippi	B	D
North Carolina	B	D
South Carolina	B	D
Tennessee	D	A–
Washington	F	C

MATH		
STATE	2005	2010
Delaware	F	B
District of Columbia	D	A
Florida	F	A
Hawaii	F	C
Idaho	D	B
Michigan	C	A–
Minnesota	D	B
Oregon	D	B+
Utah	D	A–
Washington	F	A

Source: Sheila Byrd Carmichael et al., *The State of State Standards—and the Common Core—in 2010* (Washington, DC: Thomas B. Fordham Institute, 2010), tables 2 and 3.

Note: Only states that adopted CCR standards in 2010 are included. Criteria and grading scale differed between 2005 and 2010. See appendix C in the 2010 Fordham Institute report.

Florida: An Example of State Standards Changing pre-2010

Notice that Florida's math standards went from an F to an A grade from 2005 to 2010. The state's experience with standards underscores the point that standards are constantly evolving. Florida adopted curriculum frameworks in all major academic subjects in 1985. They remained in effect until 1995. In 1996, the state adopted Florida Sunshine State

Standards along with an annual state test, the Florida Comprehensive Assessment Test (FCAT). This regime remained in effect until 2007. The Sunshine State Standards were not well regarded. The 2007 legislation demanding replacement of the standards cited the dismal grades the standards had consistently received from the Thomas B. Fordham Foundation (in math, Ds in 1998 and 2000 and, as shown in table 6.2, an F in 2005). The legislation throwing out the Sunshine State Standards mandated that new standards receive approval from "one or more nationally respected foundations, institutes, organizations, or boards with expertise in performance standards for K-12 curricula."[9]

A fresh set of Florida math standards were adopted in the fall of 2007 and ELA standards in January 2008. Dubbed Next-Generation Sunshine State Standards, the standards were reviewed by the Fordham Institute in 2010, receiving a B in ELA and an A in math. On Content and Rigor, the rating used by C-SAIL to categorize Florida's pre–Common Core standards, Florida received a 5 (out of 7) in ELA and 7 (out of 7) in math. With such high ratings, it was therefore categorized as a comparison state in the C-SAIL analysis, suggesting it had rigorous standards in place before CCSS, despite the fact that the ink was barely dry on Florida's strong standards and had been preceded by eleven years of weak ones.

If we went back to the 1990s to investigate the instability of state standards, California and Massachusetts also stand out. Both were well regarded in standards evaluations conducted in the 2000s, but those were not the states' standards in the 1990s. The two states were fierce battlegrounds in the 1990s math wars (as discussed in chapter 3). Both states overturned standards modeled after the 1989 NCTM math standards in favor of standards embracing more traditional content. The latter standards were mostly silent on pedagogy. The newly adopted standards in California (1998) and Massachusetts (2000) were strenuously opposed by groups favoring math reform, including the NCTM and other Common Core supporters, and remained in place until Common Core. To model these standards, based on a 2010 evaluation, as qualitatively similar to the 1990s standards they replaced is historically inaccurate.

State standards changed in the post-2010 period as well. Indiana, Oklahoma, and South Carolina formally rescinded their Common Core adoptions, and other states revised standards. In 2018, the Fordham Institute assessed the quality of standards in states that had revised or revoked CCSS. As shown in table 6.3, those ratings would lead to six states switching C-SAIL categories in ELA and four states in math.

The C-SAIL study does the best it can with the data available. The authors recognize that an interrupted time series analysis would be improved if the point of interruption, the time when pre-CCSS became post-CCSS, could be determined precisely. Unlike a study of the legal age to buy alcohol, in which the starting date of enforcement is stated explicitly in law, when Common Core or any other set of standards is implemented in classrooms is difficult to pinpoint. Thus, using the date of adoption as the point of interruption, while imperfect, makes sense as it is the only observable policy change. C-SAIL researchers then tracked achievement trends as they unfolded one, three, five, and seven years after adoption, which should approximately mirror degrees of implementation

TABLE 6.3   *Fordham Institute, ELA content and rigor score (on a scale of 1 to 7), post-2010 category switchers in C-SAIL analysis*

ELA				
STATE	2010	C-SAIL ASSIGNED CATEGORY	2018	WOULD NOW BE ASSIGNED TO
Kansas	4	Excluded	6	Comparison
New York	3	Treatment	5	Comparison
North Carolina	3	Treatment	5	Comparison
West Virginia	3	Treatment	5	Comparison
Tennessee	6	Comparison	4	Excluded
Virginia	6	Comparison	2	Treatment

MATH				
STATE	2010	C-SAIL ASSIGNED CATEGORY	2018	WOULD NOW BE ASSIGNED TO
Missouri	2	Treatment	4	Excluded
North Carolina	3	Treatment	5	Comparison
Oklahoma	5	Comparison	3	Treatment
Tennessee	3	Treatment	5	Comparison

Sources: Sheila Byrd Carmichael et al., *The State of State Standards—and the Common Core—in 2010* (Washington, DC: Thomas B. Fordham Institute, 2010); Solomon Friedberg et al., *The State of State Standards Post-Common Core* (Washington, DC: Thomas B. Fordham Institute, 2018).

LEE AND WU STUDY

Jaekyung Lee and Yin Wu used NAEP survey responses of school principals to measure how closely schools were following Common Core. Principals were asked the extent to which their schools' curriculum was influenced by state standards. After aggregating that variable to the state level, Lee and Wu averaged state proficiency rates for NAEP's four subject-grade combinations to create a composite achievement score. They used regression equations to investigate the effects of Common Core on student achievement and whether state performance standards (i.e., where the cut points for proficiency are set on state tests) were affected by the new standards.[10]

Lee and Wu found no difference between CCSS and non-CCSS states in NAEP gains from 2009 to 2015. They also discovered that CCSS states raised performance standards more than non-CCSS states, making it more difficult for students to score proficient on state tests; however, raising or lowering the proficiency bar was not associated with gains in student achievement, a finding consistent with previous research.[11] Lee and Wu cautioned that it was too early to render a verdict on CCSS, but added: "The findings of this study as well as previous studies raise concerns about implementation challenges and limitations of the current CCSS-based education policies."[12]

JOSHUA BLEIBERG STUDY

Joshua Bleiberg's dissertation study at Vanderbilt University found statistically significant positive effects of CCSS in fourth-grade and eighth-grade math (about 0.07 each) from 2009 to 2017. No significant effects were found in reading. Interestingly, more than half of the positive effects in math (0.04 in both grade levels) were evident by 2011. Bleiberg describes Common Core as unfolding in three stages: adoption, preparation for implementation, and implementation. He depicts 2011 as a year in which many teachers were teaching to Common Core standards, receiving professional development, and working with Common Core curricula, all activities Bleiberg considers preparation for implementation. Full implementation, according to Bleiberg, occurs when teachers raise expectations for all students. Two states completed implementation in 2012 and another ten in 2013.[13]

Bleiberg assigns states to treatment and comparison groups based on whether they were early or late implementers of CCSS, using 2013 as the differentiating year. He restricts the analysis to states whose prior standards were rated as *low rigor* based on the Fordham Institute's 2010 ratings.[14] In addition to excluding the high-rigor states, he excludes states that substantively modified standards from 2010 to 2015 or adopted standards other than CCSS. This categorization strategy is quite different from the C-SAIL study described earlier. Recall that Song and her colleagues made the high rigor states from 2010 the comparison group. The logic of Bleiberg's strategy is to compare early-implementing low-rigor states with late-implementing low-rigor states, hypothesizing that the difference in years of implementation is a strong enough discriminator to reveal effects.

Bleiberg concluded that CCSS had a small effect on math scores and no detectable effect on reading scores. In addition, he found the positive results coming from gains among socioeconomically advantaged students (those who do not qualify for free and reduced meals) and no discernible effect arising from disadvantaged students.

BROWN CENTER STUDIES

The 2014, 2015, and 2017 Brown Center Reports included analyses of Common Core using state NAEP data. The studies used an informal differences in differences approach that does not support causal findings. In the 2014 report, changes in NAEP scores of states that adopted Common Core standards were compared to scores of states rejecting them. States that adopted CCSS were categorized as strong (nineteen states) or medium (twenty-six states) implementers; the five states that rejected CCSS-M were categorized as nonadopters.

This coding scheme is referred to as *IMP11 (Dollars)* in the discussion ahead. Sorting of strong and medium implementers was based on how states reported they used federal Recovery Act dollars to implement common standards. In 2011, the federal government asked state education department officials if, as part of their implementation plans, they spent money on professional development, new instructional materials, or joining a testing consortium. The nineteen strong implementers indicated that they were spending money on all three activities. The twenty-six medium implementers did not employ at least one of the implementation strategies. Note the difference here between the depiction of professional development, acquiring curricular materials, and joining a test consortium as *implementation*, not as *preparing for implementation*, as portrayed by the Bleiberg study.

The analysis was confined to eighth-grade math. It found that strong implementers of CCSS posted slightly larger NAEP gains from 2009 to 2013 than the nonadopting states. Strong implementers gained 1.88, medium implementers 1.00, and nonadopters 0.61 scale score points. The widest difference, between strong implementers and nonadopters, was 1.27 scale score points, less than 0.03 standard deviations. That's a small, practically undetectable difference for four years of NAEP scores.[15]

In a separate analysis—and presaging the C-SAIL study's similarity index—Schmidt and Houang's five-level evaluation of states' 2009 math standards was used to examine whether subsequent progress on NAEP math assessments was related to those rankings. As with the C-SAIL study, no association was detected between the Schmidt and Houang ratings and 2009 to 2013 math gains.

IMP13 (Time) Index

The 2015 Brown Center Report introduced a new policy index based on a 2013 survey of state officials.[16] The survey asked when states planned on CCSS being fully implemented in classrooms. States that set the end of the 2012–2013 academic year or earlier as the goal for full implementation were designated *strong implementers* ($n = 12$); states reporting a goal of full implementation after 2012–2013 ($n = 34$) were designated *medium implementers*; and non–Common Core states ($n = 4$) were designated *nonadopters*.[17] In later years, this index came to be labeled *IMP13* and the previously designed index *IMP11*, their labels noting the calendar year of the surveys on which they are based. For this book, the indexes are referred to as *IMP11 (Dollars)* and *IMP13 (Time)* to remind readers of the initial sorting criteria.

IMP13 (Time) was used to evaluate progress on NAEP's fourth-grade reading test. From 2009 to 2013, strong implementers gained 1.27 scale score points, medium implementers gained 0.82, and nonadopters declined 0.24. Like the findings on eighth-grade math, the results slightly favored CCSS, but the difference between strong implementers and nonadopters, 1.51 scale score points, represents a trivial advantage. Depending on the year, this is the equivalent of 0.03 to 0.04 SDs. The difference in fourth-grade reading scores registered on the IMP11 (Dollars) index was even smaller, 1.11 points.

The 2016 Brown Center Report updated the IMP11 (Dollars) and IMP13 (Time) analyses with 2015 NAEP data. In reading, the nonadopters made larger gains from 2013 to 2015, erasing the previous advantage of CCSS states. In math, the NAEP scores of both adopters and nonadopters declined. Because the nonadopters scores declined less, again, the advantage of CCSS states evaporated.[18]

The politics of Common Core were heating up. Indiana, Oklahoma, and South Carolina had all officially rescinded adoption of CCSS, and many states were revising standards in response to political opposition. IMP13 (Time) was made a dynamic index that could respond to such policy changes, the logic being that sorting criteria based on future plans should reflect when plans change. States that rescinded CCSS were recategorized as nonadopters.[19] States that revised the standards were designated medium implementers, which did not affect those already in the medium category but led to a recategorization of states previously in the strong implementer group. The size of each implementation group in IMP13 (Time) is displayed in table 6.4. Reflecting the rebellion against Common Core that took place after 2013 (discussed in chapter 5), nonadopting states grew and strong implementers shrank in number.

Up until 2013, and in keeping with the objective of presenting simple, straightforward analyses, no effort had been made in the Brown

TABLE 6.4   *Sample size of IMP13 (Time) implementation groups, 2009–2019 (number of states, by NAEP interval)*

IMPLEMENTATION CATEGORY	2009–2013	2013–2015	2015–2017	2017–2019
Nonadopters	5	8	10	12
Medium	34	32	32	31
Strong	11	10	8	7

Source: Author's calculations.

Note: The counts are for math and include Minnesota as a nonadopter. For reading, Minnesota switches from a nonadopter to a strong implementer.

Center analyses to control for confounding factors—in particular, demographic changes in state student populations. In durations of two to four years, this is typically not a problem when analyzing changes in state test scores (it could bias cross-sectional analysis of scores from a single year) because the distribution of students among demographic groups changes slowly and, as mentioned earlier, any baseline differences are baked into the cake.[20]

Performing a valuable service for researchers, Matt Chingos and Kristen Blagg of the Urban Institute calculated regression-adjusted state NAEP scores for the entire history of the fourth- and eighth-grade assessments and posted the data library online. The adjusted scores reflect changes in racial composition, the proportion of students qualifying for free and reduced lunch, special education and English language learner status, and the age of students at time of testing. These adjusted scores were analyzed in a 2018 study. The findings are in line with prior analyses conducted with IMP11 (Dollars) and IMP13 (Time). Nonadopters and strong implementers of Common Core made indistinguishable gains on NAEP in fourth-grade reading and eighth-grade math from 2009 to 2015. A small advantage favoring Common Core states in the early years of implementation had vanished and the trend had turned against them, with losses of one to two and a half scale score points (relative to nonadopters) in the 2013 to 2015 period.[21]

The Urban Institute adjusted scores are used in a new analysis for this book, updated with 2017 and 2019 NAEP scores. NAEP score changes from 2009 to 2019 are presented in table 6.5.

A new grouping criterion is included, P/SB19 (Test), a variable indicating whether states used either of the two Common Core assessments, PARCC or SBAC, in 2019. In addition to states using PARCC or SBAC tests, states that used a substantial number of PARCC or SBAC items in crafting hybrid assessments are included in the P/SB19 (Test) count.[22] The P/SB19 (Test) coding strategy serves as a bookend to IMP11 (Dollars), with the former based on state action at the end of the 2009 to 2019 time frame and looking backward, and the latter based on state action early in the implementation of CCSS and looking forward. IMP13 (Time) remains a dynamic coding system, and the 2017 to 2019 changes for each group were added onto the 2009 to 2017 totals, even though states' assignments to groups may have changed.

TABLE 6.5   *Differences in NAEP score changes, 2009–2019 (positive figures favor strong implementers of CCSS; negative figures favor nonadopters of CCSS)*

	SCALE SCORE POINTS			STANDARD DEVIATION UNITS		
	IMP11 (DOLLARS)	IMP13 (TIME)	P/SB19 (TEST)	IMP11 (DOLLARS)	IMP13 (TIME)	P/SB19 (TEST)
Fourth-grade math	−1.3	2.2	−1.0	−0.04	0.07	−0.03
Eighth-grade math	1.5	1.2	−0.6	0.04	0.03	−0.02
Fourth-grade reading	2.2	3.6	0.7	0.06	0.09	0.02
Eighth-grade reading	4.0	2.2	1.0	0.11	0.06	0.03

Source: Calculations made from data downloaded in April 2020 from "America's Gradebook: How Does Your State Stack Up?," Urban Institute, updated March 2, 2020, https://apps.urban.org /features/naep/.

Note: NAEP scores changes reported in scale score (SS) and standard deviation (SD) units. SD units are calculated using 2019 student standard deviations: MTH4 (32), MTH8 (40), RDG4 (39), and RDG8 (38).

The results in table 6.5 contrast the NAEP changes of nonadopters and strong implementers. Only small differences are apparent. The largest NAEP gain favoring strong implementers is 4.0 scale score points using IMP11 (Dollars) as the coding strategy for eighth-grade reading. The largest difference favoring nonadopters is −1.3 points for fourth-grade math using IMP11 (Dollars) to group states. As shown in the right half of the table expressing the differences in standard deviation units, no difference exceeds 0.11 SDs, a trivial amount for a ten-year period.

It's important to point out that the results in table 6.5 are the most positive for strong implementers of CCSS since the first BCR analysis in 2013. Finding a relative strengthening of Common Core states in the latter NAEP years is the opposite of what the C-SAIL study found. In this analysis, it's because the NAEP scores of nonadopters declined substantially from 2015 to 2017 and again from 2017 to 2019. Let's not overlook the headline story: from 2009 to 2019, overall NAEP scores were flat, and neither Common Core nor non–Common Core states performed well. Consider the 4.0-point advantage of strong implementers in eighth-grade reading. Strong implementers declined 0.5 scale score points over the ten-year period, but the nonadopters' scores declined by 4.5 points.

The bottom line is that the BCR models uncover no evidence that Common Core status is associated with large achievement differences.

Strengths and Weaknesses of the Brown Center Report Studies

The strongest characteristic of the BCR studies is that by employing a differences in differences design, they control for unobserved variables that are present at the baseline (2009) and remain stable throughout the post-CCSS period. This alone, however, does not warrant considering the detected effects as causal. When Common Core standards were adopted is known, but not when they were implemented. Some states may have taken several years to fully implement CCSS in classrooms, and including NAEP scores as if the standards were in effect for years in which they were not could bias findings. Moreover, trends prior to CCSS cannot be estimated accurately because of information lacking on the content of states' standards before 2010 and when those standards were implemented.

RACE/ETHNICITY ACHIEVEMENT GAPS

One of the primary concerns of education policy is to address inequities in academic achievement among racial and ethnic groups. In particular, NAEP scores are watched closely to see if stubborn gaps associated with race and ethnicity are closing. Since the first NAEP test was given, white and Asian students have persistently outscored Black and Hispanic students in both math and reading. Tables 6.6a to 6.6d present the NAEP scores from 1990 to 2019 of the four largest racial and ethnic groups: Asian/Pacific Islanders, Blacks, Hispanics, and whites. Unlike the data from the studies summarized earlier, the data analyzed for the remainder of the chapter are unadjusted scale scores.

In all four subject-grade combinations, Asian/Pacific Islanders have the highest scores, followed by whites, Hispanics, and Blacks. All four groups made significant growth from the first year the main NAEP was given (1990 in math, 1992 in reading) to 2019. Fourth-grade math registers the most positive outcomes, with Asian/Pacific Islander students making their largest gains in the 1990s, Black and Hispanic students in the 2000s, and white students in either the 1990s or 2000s (a gain of fourteen points in each decade). To appreciate how large the gains have been in fourth-grade math, consider that many NAEP analysts

TABLE 6.6A   *Fourth-grade math, NAEP average score, by race/ethnicity, 1990–2019*

YEAR	ASIAN/PACIFIC ISLANDER	BLACK	HISPANIC	WHITE
2019	260*	224*	231*	249
2009	255	222	227	248
2000	246[a]	203	208	234
1990	225	188	200	220

Data source: NAEP Data Explorer.

*Change from 2009–2019 statistically significant, p < 0.05.

[a]Score for 2000 unavailable due to sampling standards not met. Score reported from 2003.

TABLE 6.6B   *Eighth-grade math, NAEP average score, by race/ethnicity, 1990–2019*

YEAR	ASIAN/PACIFIC ISLANDER	BLACK	HISPANIC	WHITE
2019	310*	260	268*	292
2009	301	261	266	293
2000	288	244	253	284
1990	275	237	246	270

Data source: NAEP Data Explorer.

*Change from 2009–2019 statistically significant, p < 0.05.

TABLE 6.6C   *Fourth-grade reading, NAEP average score, by race/ethnicity, 1992–2019*

YEAR	ASIAN/PACIFIC ISLANDER	BLACK	HISPANIC	WHITE
2019	237	204	209*	230
2009	235	205	205	230
2002	224	199	201	229
1992	216	192	197	224

Data source: NAEP Data Explorer.

*Change from 2009–2019 statistically significant, p < 0.05.

TABLE 6.6D   *Eighth-grade reading, NAEP average score, by race/ethnicity,*
1992–2019

YEAR	ASIAN/PACIFIC ISLANDER	BLACK	HISPANIC	WHITE
2019	281*	244*	252*	272
2009	274	246	249	273
2002	267	245	247	272
1992	268	237	241	267

Data source: NAEP Data Explorer.
*Change from 2009–2019 statistically significant, p < 0.05.

regard ten scale score points as a ballpark estimate of one year's worth of learning. As shown in table 6.6a, the largest gain was registered by Blacks, scoring 188 in 1990 and 224 in 2019, a gain of thirty-six points. A ballpark estimate, then, is that the average Black fourth grader in 2019 knows about 3.5 years' worth more of math than the average Black fourth grader did in 1990.

For the latest decade, 2009 to 2019, Hispanics registered statistically significant gains on all four NAEP assessments. Asian/Pacific Islanders made gains in both fourth- and eighth-grade math and eighth-grade reading. Black and white scores were basically flat. Blacks made a statistically significant gain in fourth-grade math but registered a statistically significant decline in eighth-grade reading. None of the changes in white scores from 2009 to 2019 were significant.

As pointed out in earlier chapters, Common Core advocates believed that CCSS would help to reduce test score gaps based on race and ethnicity. Table 6.7 examines the Black-white and Hispanic-white test score gaps in mathematics that are associated with states using and not using Common Core–aligned assessments.[23] Table 6.8 provides the same analysis for reading. Remember that these data are correlational; they do not support causal claims. They also are raw scale scores, unadjusted for changes in income or any other potential influences on achievement.

The data offer little support for the hypothesis that CCSS is associated with closing gaps. The largest difference favoring the Common Core states is in the fourth-grade Black-white gap in math, contracting by 1.1 points in states with a CCSS-aligned test and expanding by

TABLE 6.7   *Math, NAEP race/ethnicity gaps, Common Core and non–Common Core states (based on PS/B19), 2009–2019*

GAP	YEARS	COMMON CORE	NON–COMMON CORE
Black–white fourth grade	2019	24.8	25.6
	2009	25.9	24.3
	Change 2009–2019	–1.1	1.3
Black–white eighth grade	2019	34.7	31.9
	2009	34.0	28.9
	Change 2009–2019	0.7	3.0
Hispanic–white fourth grade	2019	19.3	18.7
	2009	18.8	17.9
	Change 2009–2019	0.4	0.7
Hispanic–white eighth grade	2019	24.5	21.3
	2009	25.1	22.0
	Change 2009–2019	–0.6	–0.8

Source: Author's calculations, based on NAEP Data Explorer. Numbers may not add up due to rounding. States categorized based on 2019 use of Common Core–aligned (PARCC or SBAC) or non–Common Core assessment. Coding in other analyses referred to as P/SB19 (Test).

TABLE 6.8   *Reading, NAEP race/ethnicity gaps, Common Core and non–Common Core states, 2009–2019*

GAP	YEARS	COMMON CORE	NON–COMMON CORE
Black–white fourth grade	2019	27.7	26.3
	2009	25.5	24.6
	Change 2009–2019	2.2	1.7
Black–white eighth grade	2019	29.5	27.0
	2009	26.9	24.0
	Change 2009–2019	2.5	3.0
Hispanic–white fourth grade	2019	22.9	19.6
	2009	21.8	21.0
	Change 2009–2019	1.1	–1.5
Hispanic–white eighth grade	2019	22.1	18.1
	2009	22.2	18.4
	Change 2009–2019	–0.2	–0.4

Source: Author's calculations, based on NAEP Data Explorer. Numbers may not add up due to rounding. States categorized based on 2019 use of Common Core–aligned (PARCC or SBAC) or non–Common Core assessment. Coding in other analyses referred to as P/SB19 (Test).

1.3 points in states with a non-CCSS test. That differential is the largest in table 6.7. In Common Core states, it declined from 25.9 scale score points in 2009 to 24.8 points in 2019. In non–Common Core states, it grew from 24.3 to 25.6.

The largest difference favoring non–Common Core states is in the fourth-grade Hispanic-white gap in reading, with a 1.1 point expansion in CCSS states (from 21.8 to 22.9), while a 1.5 point contraction took place in non–Common Core states. In both tables, the Hispanic-white gaps are smaller than the corresponding Black-white gaps.

THE SPREAD OF ACHIEVEMENT

Another set of gaps that analysts are interested in pertains to the spread of achievement—that is, how dispersed test scores are over time. Rising scores that are also spreading out more could indicate that not all students are taking part in learning gains. A common statistical measure of spread is a data set's standard deviation. About two-thirds of data that are normally distributed (shaped like a bell curve) fall within one standard deviation of the mean (one-third above it and one-third below). NAEP's standard deviations on all four tests widened by at least 10 percent from 2009 to 2019.

The increasing dispersion of NAEP scores is evident on the tails of the distribution—at the ninetieth and tenth percentiles. Scores at the ninetieth percentile represent the top 10 percent of scores; scores at the tenth percentile represent the bottom 10 percent. These two locations on the distribution are often used to identify, respectively, the nation's highest and lowest achievers. The size of the gap between the ninetieth and tenth percentiles has grown by about 10 percent on all four NAEP

TABLE 6.9   *NAEP standard deviations, 2009–2019*

GRADE/SUBJECT	2009	2019
Fourth-grade math	29	32
Eighth-grade math	36	40
Fourth-grade reading	35	39
Eighth-grade reading	34	38

Source: NAEP Data Explorer.

tests over the 2009 to 2019 decade, equal to eight to ten scale score points. Peggy G. Carr, associate commissioner of the National Center for Education Statistics, highlighted the phenomenon in the official release of the 2019 NAEP scores, noting that scores at the tenth percentile had fallen back to about what they were in 1990.[24]

Table 6.10 displays the growth of the ninetieth to tenth percentile gaps from 2009 to 2019, again disaggregated by whether states used or did not use a Common Core–aligned test in 2019. In both groups of states, the ninetieth to tenth percentile gap widened by about 10 percent. The increased dispersion of scores primarily occurred because of declining NAEP scores at the tenth percentile, and that was true for both Common Core and non–Common Core states. Consistent with Peggy G. Carr's point, all four grade/subject combinations in the table exhibit sharp declines at the tenth percentile.

TABLE 6.10   *Ninetieth to tenth percentile gaps, Common Core and non–Common Core states (based on PS/B19), 2009–2019*

TEST USED		COMMON CORE			NON-COMMON CORE		
GRADE/SUBJECT	YEARS	90TH	10TH	GAP	90TH	10TH	GAP
Fourth-grade math	2019	278.0	196.4	81.6	278.7	199.6	79.1
	2009	274.5	202.0	72.5	274.1	204.3	69.8
	Gap change			9.2			9.3
Eighth-grade math	2019	331.5	229.7	101.8	330.3	231.4	98.9
	2009	327.9	237.1	90.8	326.0	238.6	87.4
	Gap change			11.0			11.5
Fourth-grade reading	2019	265.5	166.2	99.3	265.0	167.8	97.2
	2009	262.2	173.7	88.5	262.2	175.9	86.3
	Gap change			10.8			10.0
Eighth-grade reading	2019	308.9	212.6	96.3	306.6	213.0	93.6
	2009	303.6	220.6	83.1	303.1	221.1	82.0
	Gap change			13.3			11.5

Source: Author's calculations, based on NAEP Data Explorer. Numbers may not add up due to rounding.

States categorized based on 2019 use of Common Core–aligned (PARCC or SBAC) or non–Common Core assessment.

In terms of 90–10 gap growth, the differences between the two groups of states are small. The largest difference is in eighth-grade reading, and even that difference is less than two scale score points.

CONCLUSION

This chapter reviewed the existing research, as of the spring of 2020, on Common Core and its impact on student achievement. The evidence is mixed in terms of finding positive or negative effects, but not mixed in terms of magnitude. All of the studies find small effects, ranging from about plus or minus one-tenth of a standard deviation—or three to four points on one of the NAEP tests. That represents a decade of effort.

The existing body of evidence does not support advocates' claims that Common Core would dramatically boost student achievement or reduce test score gaps between white students and students of color. Nor does it support claims by Common Core opponents that Common Core is responsible for the 2009 to 2019 decade of stagnation in academic achievement. The lack of progress is a real phenomenon, but it can be found in Common Core and non–Common Core states alike.

Beneath the surface of stagnant NAEP scores, the spread of achievement is broadening. Gaps between the highest and lowest achievers widened from 2009 to 2019, but that trend, too, appears to be unrelated to Common Core. Students in the bottom 10 percent of achievement are losing ground regardless of whether they go to school in states that adopted or rejected CCSS.

Let's postpone further discussion of student achievement until the book's concluding chapter. Learning is strongly connected to curriculum and instruction, and it is to those topics that we turn next.

7

EFFECTS ON CURRICULUM AND INSTRUCTION

E ven if Common Core produced no positive effect on student learning, perhaps other aspects of schooling benefitted. Before examining curriculum and instruction as key elements of teaching and learning, let's consider them as resources that must be acquired by and distributed within educational systems. One assumed benefit of the fifty states having common standards involves efficiencies in producing curricular materials, particularly textbooks. Publishers have long complained of the costs incurred from having to produce dozens of different versions of textbooks to comply with the dictates of varying state standards. Common standards should allow for perhaps not one single textbook, but certainly a smaller set of texts that could be marketed nationally. The resulting economies of scale would extend to research on textbook effectiveness as well. Researchers would have a known, limited population of materials to assess, implemented in hundreds of different schools, operating under heterogeneous conditions, taught by different teachers and serving different kids. These conditions are ideal for conducting good evaluations.[1]

How much would actually be saved by reducing the current number of textbooks? Maybe very little. The complaint that the lack of uniform standards produces too many texts replaced a long-standing charge: that two populous states—Texas and California—exercised inordinate influence over the content of other states' textbooks. This phenomenon was often called the California-Texas effect. Both states had state-level textbook adoptions throughout the twentieth century (California abandoned state adoption in 2013). Textbook critics charged that publishers initially created texts that would survive the highly politicized adoption process in those states, even if it meant sacrificing quality for political acceptance, and then tweaked the books to supply variants to other states. The complaint was that textbooks were *too similar*, not too different, leaving states other than California and Texas with no true market in which to choose curriculum materials.[2]

If all of the different versions of textbooks were fairly similar to begin with, harmonizing them further won't generate much savings. In addition, consider the track record of college texts. The same book may be priced differently in different markets. Many college texts are sold internationally. One study discovered that an organic chemistry text commonly taught in US premed programs was also available on a Canadian website. The international version was available for twelve dollars on the Canadian website, but the US hard-copy version of the exact same text cost $213 new and about $150 in used condition.[3] That suggests individual markets, not content or effectiveness or other characteristics of textbooks, drive price.

Are uniform standards more likely to promote rigorous evaluations of instructional materials that would then improve the overall quality of curricula? That too is doubtful. The most scientifically sound evaluation of multiple math textbooks was conducted by Mathematica in a randomized control trial of four programs in the first and second grades.[4] That study was conducted over a three-year period, from 2006 to 2009, and predates Common Core. The math programs varied on emphasizing student-centered or teacher-directed approaches. In first-grade classrooms, students in one of the programs, Math Expressions, scored 0.11 standard deviations higher than students in two of the other programs, Investigations and Scott Foresman-Addison Wesley Mathematics. In second-grade classrooms, Math Expressions students outscored Scott Foresman-Addison Wesley students by 0.12 standard deviations, and Saxon students did even better, outscoring Scott Foresman-Addison Wesley students by 0.17 standard deviations.

No similarly randomized studies of Common Core–aligned curricula have been performed as of the writing of this book, approximately ten years after the release of CCSS. A 2019 study by researchers affiliated with the Center for Education Policy Research examined longitudinal, student-level test score data that matched students with the math textbooks that their schools used in the fourth and fifth grades. Fifteen textbook series were dominant, comprising 90 percent of the market share in the study's six states. All six states were Common Core states. Seven textbooks were used by 70 percent of schools. The researchers found no significant differences in student achievement among the series, nor any significant differences between the textbooks aligned with Common Core and those published before Common Core.[5]

Not having sound evidence of the efficacy of curriculum is not Common Core's fault. It's not local educators' fault, either; such evidence rarely exists. Schools and districts routinely adopt textbook series without knowing whether the chosen curriculum boosts or hinders student learning, a situation Matthew M. Chingos and Grover J. "Russ" Whitehurst described as *choosing blindly* in their 2012 report of the same name.[6] In the place of evidence of effectiveness, the customary approach has been to rely on reviews.

REVIEWS OF COMMON CORE TEXTBOOKS

After states adopted CCSS, publishers responded, in the terms used by a National Public Radio report, by *rushing to flood* and *inundate* local districts with new curriculum materials.[7] Unfortunately, the new materials weren't necessarily good—or even new. William Schmidt of Michigan State University and Morgan Polikoff of the University of Southern California separately studied samples of the new textbooks and concluded that revised editions of existing math texts, often adorned with gold stickers proclaiming, "Common Core aligned," actually contained nothing new. In a 2014 presentation before the Education Writers Association, Schmidt called the publishers "snake oil salesmen" for marketing older versions of textbooks as if they had been rewritten in accordance with Common Core. Schmidt's review of thirty-four texts found that the average textbook was missing about one-fourth of the standards stipulated for any particular grade.[8] Polikoff was equally blunt about teachers' use of nonaligned texts: "If they follow the book they will not be teaching Common Core."[9]

Polikoff's review found content "not evenly allocated across objectives (as is assumed for the standards)." Polikoff went on to remark, "Indeed, a glance through the textbooks indicates that they are heavily focused on certain content areas (e.g., multiplication of multidigit numbers) and much less so on others (e.g., understanding additive properties of angles)."[10]

Some content imbalances may be built into CCSS. The math standards identify the "major work" of each grade or cluster of grades as the objectives that are most important. For third through fifth grades, the standards summarize the major work as "concepts, skills, and problem solving related to multiplication and division of whole numbers and fractions." Polikoff examined fourth-grade texts. It is well within the spirit of the standards to emphasize multiplication of multidigit numbers over the properties of angles. Student Achievement Partners published several tools to help teachers interpret the standards. The handout *Where to Focus Grade 4 Mathematics* states, "Not all content in a given grade is emphasized equally in the Standards." It divides grade-level objectives into content clusters and assigns one of three levels of importance: major, supporting, and additional clusters. The fourth-grade standards involving multiplication of whole numbers are labeled at the highest level, *major clusters*, while those involving angles are classified at the lowest level, *additional clusters*.[11]

EDREPORTS.ORG

EdReports.org was launched in 2014, establishing independent review panels of math and ELA textbooks to determine alignment with Common Core. The effort was led by Maria M. Klawe, president of Harvey Mudd College, and received funding from the Bill & Melinda Gates Foundation and several other philanthropies. About half of the reviewers are current classroom teachers, with many on the early review teams having worked with Student Achievement Partners, associated with Common Core authors.[12]

EdReports employs a "gateway" evaluation process. Let's look at math. If textbooks fail the first gateway, which is meeting or partially meeting alignment with Common Core on focus and coherence, the review ends. The second gateway is rigor and mathematical practices.

Texts passing the first two gateways go on to be reviewed for usability (the third gateway). It is defined as follows: "Degree to which materials are consistent with effective practices (as outlined in the evaluation tool) for use and design, teacher planning and learning, assessment, differentiated instruction, and effective technology use."[13]

Even programs receiving favorable reviews have raised concerns about the review process. The Charles A. Dana Center, housed at the University of Texas-Austin, created the Agile Mind math series, running from middle school through high school mathematics. The high school texts received favorable reviews, but in a few areas they were deemed as only partially meeting expectations. A prominent complaint about the Algebra I materials was that they infrequently used complex types of real numbers in favor of simpler types. The Dana Center argued that using familiar forms of numbers to introduce such concepts as linear equations and inequalities, dividing polynomials, and solving quadratic equations allows students greater accessibility to new concepts.

There is nothing unusual about this approach. Students are more confident working with whole numbers, for example, and the phenomenon known as *whole number bias* in instruction rests on the observation that encountering fractions too early in working with novel tasks may overwhelm students.[14] A student who is a little shaky with fractions might come to grasp factoring polynomials quickly when whole numbers are used but find them incomprehensible with fractions. In its response to the reviews, the publishers of Agile Mind challenged Ed Reports to cite evidence supporting some of the evaluation criteria:

We encourage *Ed Reports* to share the evidentiary basis for their evaluation criteria, to allow the field to provide additional feedback and to ensure that the criteria reflect proven, high-yield resources and practices that impact student learning and achievement. We worry that, in their current form, some *Ed Reports* criteria could overlook the promise of tools with the potential to enhance educator practice, while rewarding supports that lack evidence of impact on student learning.

An example from Gateway 1 Indicator 1c. *The materials require students to engage in mathematics at a level of sophistication appropriate to high school.* To fully meet this indicator, according to the *Ed Reports high school evidence guide,* materials must do three things. They must "regularly use age appropriate contexts, use various types of real numbers, and provide opportunities for students to apply key takeaways from grades 6-8." While the second aspect of this criterion speaks to the use of various types of real numbers, we worry that *Ed Reports* appears to be overweighting the amount of student practice with operations with a variety of number types, when compared to other aspects of this criterion . . . Our instructional materials balance students' need to maintain quantitative understanding and skills with the need to allow students to focus on mastering new mathematical concepts without introducing an added level of complexity at the outset of new learning by also asking them to address operations with a variety of types of real numbers. We believe this design principle is supportive of students as they work to develop fluency with new algebraic and geometric skills and is vital for teachers in making formative assessments of students' progress toward mastery of content.[15]

This argument is referring to *cognitive load theory,* which, as noted in chapter 4, has generated a body of supportive research. The authors of Agile Mind are arguing that they use simpler forms of numbers to introduce new concepts so as to not overload students who may lack confidence using other forms of numbers. They are also asking for the evidentiary base that suggests this approach is inferior to the criteria the reviewers are enforcing.

The EdReports review of Agile Mind also displays a bias against explicit instruction that helps students, in its view, too much. The review gives several examples of the offense:

There is a Constructed Response question on the Assessment that is an application where students are required to identify the variables, write a system, use a graph or table to solve, and then show how to check the answer. They are taken step-by-step through the process.

In Algebra I Topic 8 (A-CED.2) Student Activity Sheet 3 Question 26 is an example of an application problem where students choose their tools to use in order to solve the problem. However, there are exact values given to students leading to one correct answer.

> The Constructed Response assessment item for the topic gives students exact measurements when starting the problem, steps them through by telling them which tools to use, and does not have them justify their solution; therefore, students do not complete the modeling cycle.[16]

The terms *step-by-step* and *one correct answer* are pejoratives for a curriculum that provides guidance with explicit instruction. The Agile Mind authors defend explicit instruction as a technique for teaching students the appropriate tools for mathematical modeling, with student choice of modeling strategy coming after mastery of different approaches.

THE PROBLEM WITH ALIGNMENT

The goal of EdReports is to serve as an objective, Consumer Reports–style site for curriculum. It includes teachers in the review process and produces reports that are intended to help teachers and local educators select textbooks. The review process carefully scrutinizes textbook series, with initial deliberations focused on one question: Is this textbook aligned with CCSS? Under the gateway protocols, if the textbook is not aligned, the review is over. If it is aligned, the textbook progresses in the review process.[17]

The problem with the process is that alignment with a set of standards—any standards, not just CCSS—is a poor proxy for quality. It is a proxy for conformity, for whether the content covered in a textbook matches with objectives delineated in standards documents. Two textbooks may cover identical content, with one producing students who learn a tremendous amount and the other producing students who struggle and are confused. Moreover, as is clear from the Agile Mind review, the appropriate level of teacher expectations when standards are enacted with instruction surely depends on each student's prior mathematics knowledge.

THE STRANGE CASE OF SINGAPORE MATH

The clearest illustration of the weak relationship between alignment and effectiveness can be found in the experience of Singapore math in the EdReports process. The math standards of Singapore have been highly regarded since the island nation first scored at the top of the TIMSS league tables in 1995. Common Core advocates have stressed from the beginning that CCSS are internationally benchmarked, reflecting similar expectations as the world's leading nations in K–12 mathematics. Early in the implementation process, bloggers at The 74 and the Fordham Institute, strong supporters of Common Core, pointed to math books based on the Singapore math standards as ideal curriculum for CCSS.[18] Achieve, one of Common Core's parent organizations, published a policy brief assuring the following: "The CCSS and the Singapore Mathematics Syllabus describe expectations of comparable rigor at each grade level. The two documents contain similar expectations for what students should know and be able to do by the end of grades 4 and 8. In high school, though, the CCSS expect slightly more than the Singapore Mathematics Syllabus expects of all students."[19] But when EdReports reviewed Math in Focus and Singapore Math: Primary Mathematics Common Core Edition, two programs based on the Singapore math standards, the reviews rejected the books for containing above-grade-level materials. The review of the second-grade edition of Singapore Math: Primary Mathematics Common Core Edition begins, "The instructional materials for Primary Mathematics Common Core Edition Grade 2 do not meet expectations for assessing grade-level content. There are many assessment items that align to standards above grade level, and the omission of the items and adaptations of the materials would affect the underlying structure of the materials."

The review is accurate. Singaporean students are introduced to multiplication and division with small numbers (including 2, 3, 4, 5, and 10) in grade 2.[20] Common Core introduces multiplication in third grade. Singapore introduces money and decimal notation in grade 2, while Common Core introduces coins and dollars in second grade but delays the introduction of decimal notation until fourth grade. The very reason that some textbook analysts admire the Singapore standards is because they successfully move students quickly through material. The review supplies several instances of the textbook straying above grade level and specifies the above-grade-level Common Core standard that documents the offense. The review cites *assessment items*, but do not be confused by that. The EdReports review process allows for some above-grade-level topics to be taught so long as students are not held accountable for knowing them on an assessment; therefore, the technical violation is that above-grade-level topics were tested. They were also taught—and recall as you read excerpts from the review that the first number in the standards code identifies the grade level of the standard:

Three of the twelve Grade 2 units assess multiplication and division, which aligns to 3.OA. Unit 8 addresses money and includes decimal notation, which aligns to 4.NF.C. Unit 9 addresses fractions and assesses students on comparing and ordering fractions, which aligns to 3.NF.3d. For example:

- Unit 4, Tests A and B assess multiplication, which aligns to 3.OA.
  - ▷ Test A, Question 5, "What is the correct multiplication equation for the picture below?"
  - ▷ Test A, Question 12, "Write 2 multiplication equations for the picture below."
  - ▷ Test B, Question 9, "Write 2 multiplication equations for the picture below."
  - ▷ Test B, Question 11, "There are 7 eggs in each basket. How many eggs are there in 3 baskets?"

- Unit 4, Tests A and B assess division, which aligns to 3.OA.
  - ▷ Test A, Question 2, "Eight blocks are shared equally between 2 children. How many blocks does each child receive?"
  - ▷ Test A, Question 13, "Circle to make groups of 4. Then write a division equation."
  - ▷ Test B, Question 10, "Write 2 multiplication equations and 2 division equations for the picture below."
  - ▷ Test B, Question 13, "Fourteen tickets are shared equally among some children. Each child gets 2 tickets. How many children are there?"

- Unit 5, Tests A and B assess multiplication tables of 2 and 3 and division, which align to 3.OA.
  - ▷ Test A, Question 2, "Multiply 2 by 6. What is the answer?"
  - ▷ Test A, Question 8, "2 x ____ = 6, 6 divided by 2 = ____"

▷ Test B, Question 9, "_____ x 3 = 9, 9 divided by 3 = _____"
▷ Test B, Question 12, "Darryl has 18 guppies. He puts them equally into three tanks. How many guppies are there in each tank?"[21]

The series Math in Focus is rejected for similar transgressions. What makes that verdict particularly troubling is that Math in Focus is one of the few elementary math textbooks with evidence of effectiveness, producing an average gain of 0.18 standard deviations in three randomized trials involving about three thousand students.[22] In contrast, most series that have received glowing reviews from EdReports lack such evidence. They excel at alignment, not necessarily at learning. As Robert Slavin points out, "We once examined all of the textbooks rated 'green' (the top ranking on EdReports, which reviews textbooks for alignment with college- and career-ready standards). Out of dozens of reading and math texts with this top rating, two had small positive impacts on learning, compared to control groups."[23]

TEXT COMPLEXITY, READING SKILLS, AND TEXT-BASED INSTRUCTION

Common Core discourages leveled-reading approaches, in which texts are selected for readers based on students' reading abilities. CCSS recommend complex texts at each grade level, with teachers selecting high-quality, demanding readings and then basing instruction around them. What is a complex text? As pointed out in chapter 4, CCSS urges the use of both qualitative and quantitative criteria to select texts, suggesting statistical tools for measuring complexity. Many teachers distrust quantitative methods for evaluating texts, fearing that converting a literary characteristic into a measurable construct may lose what's important or beautiful about that trait. Obtuse prose that is fundamentally nonliterary may register as challenging and sophisticated literature as simple. Author Mike Mullen (*Ashfall*) blogged about Lexiles on the *League of Extraordinary Writers*.[24] Great works, such as Elie Wiesel's *Night* or Ernest Hemingway's *A Farewell to Arms*, score low on Lexile measures and are deemed elementary-grade texts. *Night* (570) and *A Farewell to Arms* (730) fall far short of the 955 to 1,155 Lexile range that

CCSS recommends for sixth–eighth grades. Even *Hunger Games*, popular with teens, is too simple for sixth grade, scoring 810—appropriate for fifth grade.

A consideration of what readers bring to a text is lost with Lexiles. As we discussed in chapter 4, prior knowledge matters a great deal in how much new knowledge readers can glean from a passage. E. D. Hirsch criticizes the leveled-reader systems for this oversight: "Two texts that are rated at the same difficulty level are rarely of the same difficulty for an individual student. Actual difficulty, not theoretical difficulty, is what counts. A student can be an excellent reader about dinosaurs and a terrible reader about mushrooms; the leveled-reader system is not individualistic in the one respect that it needs to be. It cannot determine the actual difficulty level of a book for an individual student, nor gauge how best to overcome the knowledge deficits that make reading difficult for that student."[25] The irony is that both Common Core and the leveled-reading approach rely on determining the level of a text—and need a metric such as Lexiles—but for different reasons. For CCSS, the tool is employed to identify what qualifies as a complex text for instructing a whole class at a particular grade level; for leveled reading, it's employed to match texts to students' reading abilities. If it is a poor way of matching an individual reader to an appropriate text, surely it does no better in matching an entire class to one.

The Fordham Institute surveyed ELA teachers in 2012 and 2017 to see how the standards were being implemented. Between 2012 and 2017, the percentage of teachers organizing their instruction around reading skills and strategies, a practice discouraged by CCSS, rose from 56 percent to 62 percent; the percentage saying they organized instruction around "particular books, short stories, essays, and poems" fell from 37 percent to 30 percent.

Contrary to CCSS precepts, the use of leveled readers also increased: "Between 2012 and 2017, the percentage of teachers who said they were more likely to choose texts based on students' grade level decreased from 38 percent to 26 percent. Conversely, the percentage who said they were more likely to base their choices on students' reading level increased from 39 percent to 57 percent. This movement toward choosing texts based on students' reading level was driven by middle and high school teachers. There was little change for elementary teachers."[26] The

RAND surveys of teachers from 2015 to 2017 contained an almost identical item and found that ELA teachers identified focusing on reading skills and strategies as aligned with their state's standards. In fact, when asked to choose which of the two approaches was more aligned with their state's standards—instruction based on skills or particular texts—approximately 75 percent named reading skills and strategies as more aligned with state standards. ELA teachers were not only doing the opposite of what Common Core wanted, they reimagined the standards to recommend something that CCSS did not recommend.[27]

FICTION AND NONFICTION

The 2016 Brown Center Report (BCR) published an analysis of Common Core's impact on curriculum and instruction. As pointed out in earlier chapters, the CCSS recommended a greater place for nonfiction in the teaching of reading, with targets set at approximately 50 percent of texts in elementary grades and 70 percent in high school. The recommendation was highly controversial.[28] Fiction has long dominated the ELA curriculum, ranging from basal readers in the early grades all the way through AP English. The BCR study examined the empirical question of whether the recommendation was penetrating to the classroom level and influencing the balance of fiction and nonfiction in literacy instruction. NAEP surveys of fourth- and eighth-grade teachers supplied the data. NAEP's survey questions were altered beginning in 2017, so the discussion ahead will focus on the original BCR analysis, which ends with 2015 results. Data from later years are provided when appropriate.

Figures 7.1 and 7.2 display data from fourth- and eighth-grade teachers from 2009 to 2015, the first few years of implementing Common Core. The dominance of fiction is most evident in 2011 as 63 percent of fourth-grade teachers reported teaching fiction to *a great extent* compared to 38 percent reporting the same emphasis for nonfiction. That twenty-five-percentage-point gap was even wider in eighth-grade classrooms in 2011, with 64 percent emphasizing fiction and 30 percent emphasizing nonfiction.

Something changed after 2011. The emphasis on fiction declined and on nonfiction increased. By 2015, the fourth-grade gap had shrunk to eight percentage points and eighth-grade gap to sixteen percentage

FIGURE 7.1   *Fourth-grade emphasis on particular types of reading*

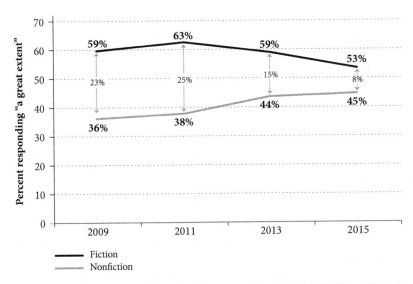

Source: Tom Loveless, "Reading and Math in the Common Core Era," *The 2016 Brown Center Report on American Education* (Washington, DC: Brown Center on Education Policy at Brookings, 2016), 9. Reprinted with permission of the Brookings Institution.

FIGURE 7.2   *Eighth-grade emphasis on particular types of reading*

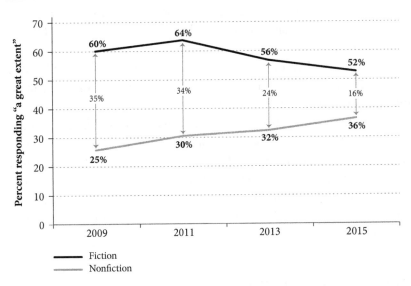

Source: Tom Loveless, "Reading and Math in the Common Core Era," *The 2016 Brown Center Report on American Education* (Washington, DC: Brown Center on Education Policy at Brookings, 2016), 9. Reprinted with permission of the Brookings Institution.

points. The study included an analysis using one of the BCR's sorting schemes—IMP13 (Time)—for categorizing states to reflect implementation of Common Core. Employing a differences in differences analysis, the study found that from 2011 to 2015, states that were strong implementers of Common Core were more likely than the nonadopters of Common Core to tip the balance toward nonfiction in the fourth grade. The difference was negligible in the eighth grade. The analysis cannot establish causality, but the association is interesting and in the direction one would expect considering the enormous effort to implement CCSS.

Do not forget that when the fiction-nonfiction controversy broke in 2012, Common Core supporters were quick to point out that the expectation for more nonfiction and informational reading was to be shared with science and history teachers, not shouldered by ELA teachers alone. Fourth-grade teachers typically instruct self-contained classes; that is, they teach the same children all day in all subjects. Maintaining a balance of fiction and nonfiction reading during the school day is their task alone. In middle and high schools, on the other hand, subjects are typically departmentalized, with students moving from science class to English class to history class, and so on, each class taught by a different teacher who is credentialed to teach that particular subject. Coordination of reading materials among several teachers is necessary to alter the overall balance.

The Fordham Institute's surveys of ELA teachers conducted in 2012 and 2017 confirm that teachers shifted away from fiction in favor of informational and literary nonfiction texts. The 2017 survey also indicated that teachers were teaching fewer classic works of literature than in the past. Almost three-fourths of elementary (73 percent) and middle school (74 percent) teachers said that they strongly agreed or somewhat agreed that they were teaching "fewer classic works of literature because there is no longer room for them in the curriculum." Support for the statement was positive but not as strong among high school teachers (53 percent).[29]

GEOMETRY AND DATA

In mathematics, CCSS place less emphasis on geometry and data analysis in the fourth grade compared to many of the previous state standards.

TABLE 7.1   *The role of geometry and data in fourth-grade math (percentage of students with teachers reporting heavy emphasis)*

	2009	2011	2013	2015
Geometry	36	36	31	29
Data	31	30	24	23

Sources: 2016 Brown Center Report; NAEP Data Explorer.

What were the national trends on fourth-grade teachers' emphasis of these topics?

Geometry and data analysis were two of the five strands in which the 1989 NCTM standards organized content. Common Core gave these two strands less importance in K–6 math in favor of a greater emphasis on numbers and operations, especially operations with whole numbers and fractions. As shown in table 7.1, a plateau in the percentage of fourth-grade students with teachers placing a heavy emphasis on geometry and data occurred from 2009 to 2011 (combined total of 66 to 67 percent), and then the proportion tailed off. By 2015, the share was down to 52 percent.

EIGHTH-GRADE MATH COURSES

A particularly contentious issue for Common Core involves math courses taken in the eighth grade. In the 1990s and 2000s, a national movement argued that all students should take an algebra course no later than the eighth grade. Robert Moses, who was awarded a MacArthur Foundation Fellowship in 1982, declared learning algebra "the new civil right," and a push for algebra courses for eighth and ninth graders spread across the country. In the late 1990s, the policy impetus culminated with the Clinton administration making eighth-grade algebra a national goal. Advanced math courses showed disproportionately low numbers of enrolled Black and Hispanic students. The campaign known as Algebra for All stressed that Algebra I was serving as a gatekeeper course holding back disadvantaged students and students of color. Encouraging students to take an Algebra I course as early as possible served the cause of equity.[30]

The campaign was remarkably successful. From 1990 to 2007, the percentage of eighth graders in Algebra I courses nearly doubled, from 16 to 31 percent. About 5 percent were even taking Algebra I in seventh grade. The movement's success produced a growing unease, however, as some observers worried that students who were unprepared for algebra were being pushed into the course too early and then, given the traditional hierarchy of high school mathematics, forced to struggle through a sequence of courses for several years. A Brown Center study analyzed student-level NAEP data and found that 28.6 percent of eighth graders scoring at the tenth percentile or below (the bottom 10 percent in the country) were taking an advanced math class (algebra or higher) in 2005. These students' math functioning was three to four years below grade level, most having little to no understanding of fractions or other forms of rational numbers. Later studies from North Carolina and Chicago found that low-achieving eighth and ninth graders did not benefit, and were probably harmed, by taking Algebra I in eighth grade and later accelerated math classes for which they were unprepared.[31]

The CCSS in math lay out a single eighth-grade math course, with content resembling a prealgebra course, followed by Algebra I in ninth grade. Appendix A to the standards suggests a "compacting" strategy as an option for accelerating precocious math students, in which they complete three years of the Common Core curriculum (seventh- and eighth-grade math and Algebra I) in two years of schooling, seventh and eighth grades. The appendix explains: "Based on a variety of inputs and factors, some students may decide at an early age that they want to take Calculus or other college level courses in high school. These students would need to begin the study of high school content in the middle school, which would lead to Precalculus or Advanced Statistics as a junior and Calculus, Advanced Statistics or other college level options as a senior."[32]

As displayed in table 7.2, enrollment in advanced math classes appears to have peaked in 2013. Enrollment in a general eighth-grade math course increased significantly in 2015, in accord with CCSS. The data are from a NAEP student survey asking students to note the course they are currently taking. Response options to this question changed after 2015, so the trend evident in table 7.2 cannot be linked to 2017 and 2019 data; however, with that caveat in mind, be aware that in 2017 and 2019, 59 percent of eighth graders said they were taking a general

TABLE 7.2   *Enrollment in eighth-grade math courses (percentage of students)*

	2000	2005	2009	2011	2013	2015
Advanced	27	42	44	47	48	43
General 8	38	25	25	25	26	32
Difference	−11	17	19	22	22	11

Sources: 2016 Brown Center Report; NAEP Data Explorer.

Note: *Advanced* includes Algebra I, Geometry, and either the first or second year of a two-year algebra sequence. *General 8* consists of either eighth-grade or basic math.

eighth-grade math course, and 39 percent said they were taking Algebra I or Geometry. This evidence suggests that a general eighth-grade math course has pushed aside Algebra I to become, as CCSS intended, the dominant math course of American eighth graders.

COGNITIVE DEMAND

Educators have been ranking different types of learning for a long time. Bloom's taxonomy is probably the most well-known attempt to organize learning by categorizing objectives. It comprises six levels—recall, comprehension, application, analysis, synthesis, and evaluation—with the complexity increasing at each level.[33] Another is Norman L. Webb's depth of knowledge levels. The tool Polikoff used to review texts, the Surveys of Enacted Curriculum, was based on research from the University of Wisconsin and influenced by Bloom's and Webb's taxonomies.[34]

The Common Core math standards define *rigor* as consisting of three types: procedures, conceptual understanding, and problem application. This is a peculiar definition of rigor because the three categories have a long history in K–12 math education as types of mathematical knowledge and a way of organizing math assessments to ensure coverage of different kinds of skill. Both difficult and easy problems can be posed within each of the three types. For several decades, the Iowa Test of Basic Skills has assessed math students in computation, concepts, and problem solving.[35] Similarly, from 1996 to 2003, NAEP mathematics items reflected three dimensions of mathematics ability: procedures, concepts, and problem solving.[36] These three dimensions, no matter what they are called, do not necessarily have anything to do with the conventional meaning of the word *rigor*. In CCSS, the dimensions are not presented as hierarchical; instead, math teachers are urged to pursue them "with equal intensity."

The term *cognitive demand* is not used in CCSS, although it is mentioned, along with *higher-order skills* and *deep conceptual understanding*, as criteria guiding the development of CCSS.[37] Media coverage of Common Core often stresses that the standards are more demanding than American schools have ever experienced before. In particular, the math standards are claimed to give greater emphasis to conceptual knowledge than past standards. Unfortunately, the belief that curricula with higher cognitive demand leads to greater math achievement is based on thin empirical evidence. One of the most frequently cited works is a 1996 study by Mary Kay Stein and Suzanne Lane, an observational study of only four schools, with student achievement measured by a researcher-designed, eleven-item math test.[38]

Andrew C. Porter of the University of Pennsylvania led a team of analysts that compared the cognitive demand of CCSS to that of previous state standards: "Our research shows that the common-core standards do not represent a meaningful improvement over existing state standards. To be sure, when we consider state standards in the aggregate, the common-core standards present a somewhat greater emphasis on higher-order thinking. But the keyword here is *somewhat*; the difference is small, and some state standards exceed the common core in this respect."[39] The researchers also compared CCSS to standards of high-achieving nations, which led Porter to question whether the push for higher-order skills may be misplaced:

> Reformers, myself included, have been saying that U.S. schools need to teach more higher-order thinking skills if we're going to catch up with other countries' educational systems. But curricula in top-performing countries we studied—like Finland, Japan, and New Zealand—put far less emphasis on higher-order thinking, and far more on basic skills, than does the common core. We need to ask ourselves: Could our enthusiasm for teaching higher-order skills possibly have gone too far? Clearly, both basic skills and higher-order thinking are important, but what is the right balance?[40]

The title of a 2015 study conducted by Harvard researchers, *Teaching Higher*, encapsulates the prevailing view that Common Core challenged teachers to "teach higher." Teachers in five Common Core states (Delaware, Maryland, Massachusetts, New Mexico, and Nevada) were surveyed on how their teaching had changed under the new standards.[41]

As shown in table 7.3, math teachers reported several changes compatible with Common Core. More than three-fourths reported an increased emphasis on conceptual understanding (81 percent) and applications (78 percent). Only 39 percent said they increased their emphasis on procedural skills, 34 percent said there had been no change, and 26 percent reported decreasing such emphasis. In ELA, more than 80 percent of teachers reported more writing assignments with evidence use and reading assignments with nonfiction. Nearly three out of ten teachers (29 percent) decreased writing assignments on real or imaginary experiences, and a similar proportion decreased the use of literature in reading (28 percent).

These figures indicate that some of Common Core's big ideas about curriculum and instruction were penetrating to the classroom level.

TABLE 7.3   *Teaching Higher survey, teachers' reports of instructional changes (percent)*

SUBJECT	APPROACH	INCREASED	DID NOT CHANGE	DECREASED
MATH	Emphasis on conceptual understanding	81	16	3
	Emphasis on applications	78	17	4
	Emphasis on procedural skills	39	34	26
ELA	Assigned writing with use of evidence	86	12	2
	Assigned writing on real/imaginary experiences	42	30	29
	Use of nonfiction in reading assignments	85	13	2
	Use of literature in reading	38	34	28

Source: Adapted from Thomas J. Kane et al., *Teaching Higher: Educators' Perspectives on Common Core Implementation* (Cambridge, MA: Center for Education Policy Research, 2016), figure 8.

DOG WHISTLES AND POLITICAL COVER

Change is not welcomed by all, especially if it touches upon old ideological disputes. As described in chapter 2, the bitter curriculum battles of the 1990s undermined the Clinton administration's national standards project. The Common Core authors desperately wanted both sides on board. Some of the standards contain subtle cues, otherwise known as *dog whistles*, somewhat hidden but evident to downstream implementers. The loudest complaints came from critics of progressive pedagogy. Barbara Oakley, an engineering professor at Oakland University, published op-eds in the *Wall Street Journal* and the *New York Times* in 2014 that took issue with Common Core's press for greater conceptual understanding. She explained her qualms in an extended essay in *Nautilus*, zeroing in on the standards' call for emphasizing conceptual understanding, procedural skills, and application equally in math instruction:

> Despite the fact that procedural skills and fluency, along with application, are supposed to be given equal emphasis with conceptual understanding, all too often it doesn't happen. Imparting a conceptual understanding reigns supreme—especially during precious class time. The problem with focusing relentlessly on understanding is that math and science students can often grasp essentials of an important idea, but this understanding can quickly slip away without consolidation through practice and repetition . . . If you use the procedure a lot, by doing many different types of problems, you will find that you understand both the why and the how behind the procedure very well indeed. The greater understanding results from the fact that your mind constructed the patterns of meaning. Continually focusing on understanding itself actually gets in the way.[42]

In the case of conceptual understanding, *equal intensity* can be translated by a reform-oriented local administrator as, "it's never received equal emphasis, so feel free to emphasize it all you want to make up for that." Another example of a CCSS dog whistle is organizing a high school math curriculum into integrated math courses (typically named Math I, Math II, and Math III) instead of the traditional Algebra, Geometry, Algebra II sequence. Integrated high school courses have long been the dream of reformers. Common Core authors offered political cover for integrated math supporters by writing standards that could be used for either approach. Fewer than 5 percent of US high school students were enrolled in integrated math courses when the standards were written, but CCSS implied an equivalency.

Georgia introduced integrated courses in 2008, urging but not forcing districts to offer them. Always controversial, the integrated course sequence was in trouble when the state adopted CCSS in 2010, but state officials used the tacit endorsement of CCSS as political cover and converted the local option into a mandate. That warrant weakened once the Common Core came under fire. The state mandate was revoked in 2015, allowing Georgia's local districts to choose the sequences of their liking. A final nail in the coffin of the policy was a survey of the state's high school math teachers revealing that 84 percent preferred the traditional sequence.[43]

NAEP last surveyed twelfth graders in 2015. When students were asked if they had taken integrated Math III in mathematics, which is the final year of the three-year series and typically taken as a junior, only 5 percent of students reported having taken the course. Integrated math does not appear to have caught on nationally, even with Common Core's implicit approval.[44]

CONCLUSION

This chapter examined the impact of Common Core on curriculum and instruction. Several classroom practices have changed in a manner consistent with CCSS. Teachers give less emphasis to fiction in ELA instruction and greater attention to nonfiction and informational texts. Fourth-grade teachers focus less on geometry and data analysis in teaching math. Fewer students take Algebra I in eighth grade and more take a general eighth-grade math class. Math instruction has shifted to a greater emphasis on conceptual understanding and applications and less emphasis on learning procedures. Teachers assign more writing tasks requiring the use of evidence instead of asking students to write imaginary stories or personal accounts.

Some trends are also contrary to CCSS. Teachers continue to select texts based on students' ability to read them instead of finding challenging texts for a particular grade level and then building whole-class instruction around those readings. Instruction on generic reading skills continues to dominate ELA instruction.

EdReports.org screened textbooks for their compatibility with Common Core and, if found in alignment, the series were evaluated on additional criteria. The process was structured to establish not just a floor for curriculum but also a ceiling. Two textbook series based on the internationally renowned math standards of Singapore, *Math in Focus* and *Singapore Math: Primary Mathematics Common Core Edition*, were found to include too many above-grade-level topics and were deemed out of alignment with CCSS. *Math in Focus* was rejected despite evidence of effectiveness in randomized control trials. Faced with students varying in preparation for CCSS's grade-level expectations, teachers have sought supplementary materials to augment instruction.

Common Core appears to have influenced curriculum and instruction, but, as we discussed in the context of studies of achievement scores in chapter 6, little evidence exists that the standards affected student achievement. I'd like to bring those two threads together in the concluding chapter and also, drawing on other lessons presented in the course of the book, discuss some of the reasons Common Core has failed to achieve its primary goal of boosting student learning.

WHATEVER HAPPENED
TO COMMON CORE?

The selling of Common Core included two little white lies. The project was an ambitious effort to raise achievement in US schools, first by setting high expectations for learning in mathematics and English language arts, and second by aligning curriculum, instruction, and other core components of schooling to those outcomes. That is the basic theory of standards-based reform. But from the start, advocates of Common Core insisted that CCSS was not a curriculum—a choice that would be left to state and local officials—and that it did not dictate instructional strategies, a decision left to teachers. Those assurances still exist on the Common Core website. They are technically true. The little white lie part is that standards are nothing absent their effect on what students are taught and how students are taught it. If the standards' ultimate learning objectives are truly a change from the status quo, they cannot be achieved without fundamentally changing K–12 curriculum and instruction.

With that in mind, let's revisit the questions posed in the introduction to this book and see how they were answered.

WHERE DID COMMON CORE COME FROM?

First, the simple answer. Three organizations—the Chief State School Officers, National Governors Association, and Achieve—organized the drafting of the Common Core State Standards (CCSS). All but five states subsequently adopted the standards for both ELA and math. Minnesota adopted the ELA standards but not the math standards.

The fuller answer places CCSS in a historical context. Common Core tried to amend the perceived flaws of No Child Left Behind, the last big effort at education reform. Allowing states to write their own standards, to design their own assessments, and to set their own thresholds for acceptable student performance were seen as mistakes of NCLB. Requiring 100 percent proficiency by 2014 was a disastrous requirement of the law, guaranteeing that almost every school in the country would be seen as a failure. Common Core would fix these problems by establishing a common set of standards, kicking the assessment can down the road, and bypassing accountability completely.

The Common Core era extended standards-based reform into its third decade of policy experimentation, but with a unique blend of the strategy's key components. Common Core–aligned assessments were eventually produced by two consortia of states. After the Every Student Succeeds Act was signed into law in 2015, the mix of standards, assessments, and accountability in the Common Core era reverted to a pattern closer to the 1990s than the 2000s. States relinquished authority over designing assessments and determining proficient student performance on the new tests, ceding control to PARCC and Smarter Balanced, but the consortia fell apart within a few years. States went their own way on testing, although the requirement that assessments be given annually in the third through eighth grades continued. The punitive aspects of NCLB were replaced by softer, gentler forms of accountability, with a focus on identifying low-achieving schools and channeling resources toward improvement. States could get tough if they so decided, but that decision was not going to be compelled by the federal government. Adopting college- and career-ready standards and administering annual tests are the main requirements of ESSA.[1]

A longer view of history allows us to see the Common Core era as the latest evolutionary stage in the regulation of schools. As described in chapter 1, the rise of the state's role in education included efforts to influence what was taught and learned in classrooms. Textbook adoptions, required courses, the rational organization of learning objectives into a sequenced curriculum, assessments that measured how much students learned—all these became conduits of influence designed to penetrate the schoolhouse walls and shape what students learned. Reports from two illustrious commissions, the Committee of Ten in 1892 and the Commission on the Reorganization of Secondary Education in 1918, bracketed a period of debate between advocates of a traditional liberal arts education and educational progressives advocating less bookish, more pragmatic learning objectives. Scholars specializing in curriculum, instruction, assessment, and school administration introduced scientific principles to activities that had been the sole province of teachers and local school leaders. States possessed nothing close to the powers they have today, especially considering the leverage that accompanies providing 40 percent of contemporary K–12 funding, but by 1930 the basic architecture for regulating curriculum and instruction was in place.

DID COMMON CORE HAVE AN EFFECT?

The CCSS succeeded in changing some aspects of American schooling, but as of this book's completion in October 2020, no convincing evidence had been produced to document a significant impact on student achievement. Common Core fell short of its promise to dramatically boost learning. It also appears to have had no significant impact on achievement gaps between racial and ethnic groups, nor a discernible effect on the distribution of achievement—in particular, NAEP score differences between high- and low-achieving students as demarcated by the ninetieth and tenth percentiles.

These findings also mean that there is no persuasive evidence that CCSS produced negative effects. NAEP scores were stagnant from 2009 to 2019, an unusually long period of time, but there is no strong evidence that Common Core was the cause. Scores were flat in both Common Core and non–Common Core states. Nationally, NAEP revealed a widening spread in achievement between high- and low-achieving students, but, again, Common Core and non–Common Core states exhibited similar trends. Students in the tenth percentile are struggling in almost all states, regardless of Common Core status. Common Core has disappointed both its most ardent supporters, who saw an educational renaissance in store for the country, and its bitterest opponents, who saw a looming disaster.

So what *did* Common Core change? Teacher surveys indicate that CCSS altered several aspects of curriculum and instruction. Teachers of ELA are reporting that they emphasize fiction less and nonfiction more in reading assignments. They have also increased the frequency of assignments that ask students to use evidence in their writing and decreased the amount of time devoted to composing stories or to writing personal accounts, such as the classic back-to-school writing assignment, "What I Did over Summer Vacation." Math teachers report that they are emphasizing conceptual understanding and applications more and procedural skills less than before Common Core. Fourth-grade teachers are giving geometry and data analysis less emphasis. Eighth-grade students are less likely to take Algebra I and are more likely to enroll in an eighth-grade math course.

Those are all shifts intended by CCSS; nevertheless, some practices discouraged by Common Core are still prevalent. Teachers continue to use leveled readers and assign texts based on students' reading levels. Instruction on reading skills, such as finding the main idea of a passage, continue to dominate instruction instead of teachers organizing lessons around challenging literary fiction and nonfiction that teachers have chosen for the whole class. Textbooks aligned with Common Core have failed to penetrate most classrooms, with only 16 percent of materials used in ELA and 26 percent of materials used in math rated highly by EdReports.org. Teachers are frequently using the internet to find instructional materials, typically with general Google searches, along with regular visits to sites such as Pinterest and Teachers Pay Teachers. The quality of downloaded materials is considered uneven at best, and one review concluded almost two-thirds should not be used at all.[2]

Adding up all of these outcomes, the documented impact of Common Core on curriculum and instruction is consistent with the finding of no significant effect overall on student achievement. Existing research does not show that the instructional changes that have occurred are consistently related to significant increases in student learning. The programs that have been endorsed by EdReports but mostly ignored by classroom teachers lack evidence of effectiveness as well.

WHAT WAS THE COMMON CORE DEBATE ABOUT?

Common Core got into political trouble long after its supporters had celebrated political victory. The standards were written, released to bipartisan praise, and adopted by most states. Two consortia of states worked to develop assessments aligned to the standards. Implementation seemed to be proceeding smoothly. States doled out money to local districts so that professional development sessions could bring local educators up to speed on the content of the standards and the new expectations for student learning. Polls showed that teachers felt positively about Common Core. And as Rick Hess pointed out in his study of early media coverage of the standards, Common Core flew below the media's radar: there was no extensive coverage, pro or con.

Then there were troubles. It became apparent in early 2013 that the opposition to CCSS that had simmered for months was spreading beyond Tea Party activists and alt-right conservatives on talk radio. The next two years were not good for Common Core's reputation. Bad math problems started circulating on social media, attracting ridicule from exasperated parents. An antitesting movement that urged parents to withdraw children from state tests gained strength in New York and spread to other states. Teachers unions toned down their earlier support of CCSS, in some cases withdrawing it completely, as the threat of teacher evaluations tied to Common Core assessments became a reality.[3]

The philosophical tug-of-war between progressives and traditionalists also surfaced. Adding to Barbara Oakley's charge that conceptual understanding was crowding out other important aspects of learning math (covered in chapter 7), Katharine Beals and Barry Garelick, writing in the *Atlantic*, describe how the math standards took conceptual understanding "to a whole new level" by requiring students to explain how they solve even simple problems. Beals and Garelick illustrate how tedious and pedantic this requirement can be in practice:

> Consider a problem that asks how many total pencils there are if five people have three pencils each. In the eyes of some educators, explaining why the answer is 15 by stating, simply, that 5 x 3 = 15 is not satisfactory. To show they truly understand why 5 x 3 is 15, and why this computation provides the answer to the given word problem, students must do more. For example, they might draw a picture illustrating five groups of three pencils. (And in some instances, as was the case recently in a third-grade classroom, a student would be considered to not understand if he or she drew three groups of five pencils.)[4]

What must have been disappointing for Common Core developers is that they had gone to great pains to fashion a compromise between the traditionalist and progressive camps when writing the standards. But as Louisa Moats noted concerning the ELA standards, political compromises embedded in the wording of the standards unraveled in implementation: "Our CCSS guidelines, conferences, publishers' materials, and books have turned away from critical, research-based methodologies on how to develop the basic underlying skills of literacy. Systematic, cumulative skill development and code-emphasis instruction is getting short shrift all around, even though we have consensus reports from the 1920's onward that show it is more effective than comprehension-focused instruction."[5]

Moats is not the only person who detected code-emphasis instruction getting too little attention. In 2019, Emily Hanford of APM Reports produced a series on flawed approaches to reading instruction, including disproven cueing strategies taught as decoding strategies in balanced literacy approaches.[6] Also in 2019, *Education Week* surveyed reading teachers in kindergarten through second grade, identified the five most widely used programs in literacy instruction, and found "many instances in which these programs diverge from evidence-based practices for teaching reading or supporting struggling students."[7]

WHY DID COMMON CORE FAIL?

Standards are aspirational documents; they look quite different than authors intend when realized in schools and classrooms. A large body of implementation research, much of it predating the standards movement, supports this point. As discussed in chapter 2, in the 1970s, Paul Berman and Milbrey McLaughlin used the term *mutual adaptation* to describe the way in which teachers and school principals bend and shape upper-level policies to fit the practicalities of classrooms. Deborah Loewenberg Ball and David K. Cohen studied elementary teachers implementing the innovative 1985 California math framework, paying close attention to instruction intending to teach higher-order thinking, as called for by the state. They found a few teachers who were receptive to the reform, but most did not substantively change their instruction.

The system has too many layers—state, district, schools, classrooms—to guarantee smooth organizational transmission from statehouse to schoolhouse. Moreover, political opposition can arise at any level, offering multiple opportunities for opponents to block reform. As discussed in chapter 5, once the standards entered schools in the form of new curricula and new ways of teaching, opposition began to grow. Several states, especially those with Republican control of the state government, reconsidered their original adoptions and rescinded the standards. In Oklahoma, the legislature had been left out of the initial adoption and reasserted its authority by reversing the adoption.

Political opposition may emerge at the local level too. Educators in districts and schools typically are not monolithic in ideologies; both traditionalists and progressive reformers occupy positions of authority. As new standards are interpreted and local resources deployed to implement them, fragmentation occurs. Conflict arises between competing views of what the standards look like in practice. After studying systemic reform in several states in the 1990s, David K. Cohen observed that when it comes to curriculum and instructional reform, local stakeholders can be united and in favor of the reform (implementation goes well), united and opposed to the reform (the reform is dead on arrival), or harbor a mix of supporters and opponents (implementation is fragmented and may incite conflict).

Cohen offered a general observation about top-down, systemic reform: "Systemic reformers have acted as though government could create new standards and pedagogy oriented to critical thinking and intellectual independence without making allowances either for the historic divisions in American opinion or for Americans' appetite for mortal combat about these issues. Like the curriculum reforms of the late 1950s and early 1960s, systemic reform was advocated by mostly education professionals and members of political elites. As many observers noted, it had no 'popular roots.'"[8] Parents may join the opposition, as noted in chapter 5, with controversial math problems circulating on social media. Parent groups opposed the conversion to integrated math classes in several districts. San Mateo, California, parents organized when they heard that middle schools were no longer going to offer an eighth-grade Algebra I course.[9] Parents in Wake County, North

Carolina, opposed the district's use of the Mathematics Vision Project, a reform-oriented math curriculum that received favorable reviews from EdReports for alignment with CCSS. In 2019, the publisher of the program sued one of the parent organizers of the protest, claiming libel, slander, and "tortious interference with business relations."[10] The lawsuit was later dropped.

LESSONS FOR FUTURE POLICY AND RESEARCH

Let me be clear. Changing Common Core to make the standards more palatable to those who have opposed them in the past will not fix the barriers to smooth implementation. The problem is inherent to top-down efforts at controlling curriculum and instruction. This is not a problem that another set of standards can solve. If standards came out tomorrow, and I agreed with every single word in them, I would still give them only a slim chance of being faithfully implemented—and less than that of moving the needle on student achievement.

You might be thinking, "Okay, Common Core failed, and success was probably a longshot from the start. Standards probably won't work. Then what should policymakers do?" From the experiences of the Common Core era, five principles stand out for future policy and research.

Principle 1: Scrap Standards-Based Reform

The idea of standards-based reform should be abandoned. It doesn't work. The basic theory is suspect. Expecting more from students by exposing them to more challenging coursework does not necessarily lead to more learning. A study of 140,000 students in Missouri found no effect of greater access to science, technology, engineering, and mathematics (STEM) courses in high school on postsecondary enrollment or degree attainment in STEM fields.[11] A study of the Michigan Merit Curriculum, which provided a college-preparatory curriculum to all students, found only a small effect in science (0.2 standard deviations), no effect in other subjects, and the suggestion of a small negative impact on high school graduation rates of students who were struggling academically when they entered high school.[12] As noted in chapter 7, studies of policies promoting Algebra I for all eighth graders found a similar pattern of results, raising alarms about placing students into coursework for which they are not adequately prepared.

That does not mean education standards or high expectations are bad ideas, but to be effective, they must be compatible with students' prior learning. They may also have to be connected to people. It could be that standards that take place organically—essentially, that evolve between parent and child in the home or between teacher and student in the classroom—produce good outcomes, but standards that occur through exogenous force or pressure—in this case, policy-induced expectations—have no effect. The analogy is to vitamins. The science is convincing that the intake of vitamins enhances health, but study after study of dietary supplements—that is, vitamins in pill form rather than in their natural state—show zero effects. If taken in excess, supplements may even be harmful.[13] Critics have charged that the billions of dollars consumers spend on vitamins is a total waste, with no impact on well-being. The same may be true of education standards. Standards imposed by policy are a poor substitute for the expectations of adults conveyed through real human relationships with children.

Principle 2: Standards Must Be Flexible

Notice that in the previous paragraph I said standards that *evolve* may produce good outcomes. Standards between people are not set in concrete. They are adapted as circumstances change. The work of bureaucracies is conducted through rules and regulations. Policies are encoded in formal documents with carefully chosen words. They consist of rules and regulations. In the comedy series *The Big Bang Theory*, Sheldon Cooper was constantly drawing up multipage legal agreements for his friends (and even his future wife) to sign. These episodes got a huge laugh because of the social ineptitude inherent in treating personal relationships in such a formal manner.

People whose jobs entail working directly with people they serve—teachers, social workers, cops—are sometimes called *street—level bureaucrats*.[14] They function within bureaucratic organizations with standard operating procedures and myriad rules and regulations that everyone is expected to follow. But street-level bureaucrats are also expected to use discretion, sometimes bending the rules when the situation demands it.

The ability to do this well, to adapt to situational imperatives, is one of the traits that separates the excellent teacher or cop from the merely average one.

Some of the problems encountered by CCSS indicate that the standards were often too rigid, forcing teachers to either reinterpret them or to seek nonaligned materials to accommodate students' needs. Recall from chapter 4 the experience of the Teach to One curriculum in Elizabeth, New Jersey, a program designed to place students in a math program tailored to their prior knowledge. Kids above or below grade level studied math out of sync with Common Core, but they were snapped back to grade level in preparation for the CCSS-aligned math assessment. Struggling students then saw math that was incomprehensible. Precocious students spent time studying math they already knew.

When teachers are asked to list the major challenges faced when implementing Common Core, two rise to the top: addressing the diversity of student abilities in the classroom and dealing with students who are unprepared for the grade-level standards teachers are compelled to teach.[15] These hindrances both suggest that standards need to be flexible and, when necessary, subordinated to the realities of classroom life. The argument that standards, curriculum, instruction, assessment, accountability, and other key components of educational systems should all be aligned sounds good in theory, but it does not follow that alignment must take place at the top of the system and be imposed downward. Teachers, working with students and parents and governed by competent administrators, may be in the best position to coordinate key elements of education so as to maximize learning.

Principle 3: Evaluate Assessment and Accountability Systems

Recall from chapter 4 that the CCSS-ELA document refers to standards as *signposts*. It is difficult to argue with how helpful good signage can be to a traveler. Assessments are one of the key indicators used to gauge student learning, and with public schools governed by voters and funded by taxpayers, assessment and accountability will probably always be part of school systems. This book devotes an entire chapter to curriculum and instruction, the primary targets of academic standards, but accountability and assessment systems are also part of standards-based reform and deserve a brief look.

As this book was being completed, the COVID-19 pandemic had put assessment and accountability systems on hold. Schools closed in the spring of 2020 and instruction moved online. State tests were cancelled. Some school campuses opened in the fall, some schools provided only online instruction, and some offered a hybrid approach with a mix of in-person and online instruction. It is difficult to tell how or if testing will proceed in the 2020–2021 school year. Once testing resumes, several problems must be resolved. The state consortia formed to create assessments aligned with Common Core have dwindled in number of members. PARCC essentially no longer exists as a state consortium, but its bank of test items has been absorbed by New Meridian, a nonprofit organization in Austin, Texas, and PARCC items are used by some states.[16] Fifteen states are still part of the Smarter Balanced consortium. For the 2017–2018 school year (the last year for which national data are available), the high school Smarter Balanced test reported 32.9 percent of students scoring at levels 3 and 4 in math, considered passing, and 50.1 percent scoring at the same levels in ELA.[17] Data on the number of students passing both subjects are not reported, but a reasonable estimate is that fewer than 30 percent of high school students were deemed college and career ready based on Smarter Balanced test scores.

That small percentage of passing students makes consequential accountability politically untenable. States will not force 70 percent of students to repeat grades; they will not deny diplomas to 70 percent of high school seniors. Sherman Dorn has described how Arizona's accountability system fell when too many students failed, especially in suburban schools.[18] In Smarter Balanced states, the conundrum that policymakers now face is that they are wedded to an unrealistic set of expectations. Once the pandemic recedes, they will have to go back to the drawing board and ask whether they have the right standards, the right assessments, and the right cut points set on those assessments for determining adequate student performance. Otherwise, the state's assessment and accountability systems will not be taken seriously.

Principle 4: Make Teaching Easier and More Effective

Hints of trouble emerged early in CCSS implementation. Educators did not regard the need for higher standards with the same urgency as the Common Core developers. They felt schools already had high standards. The 2012 Met Life Survey of the American Teacher summarized the situation as follows:

> Even prior to the implementation of Common Core, educators generally believed in the importance of high expectations and high standards for all students, and also that teachers in their school held students to high standards. Survey findings in 2010 showed that nine in 10 middle and high school teachers believed that their schools had "clearly defined and set specific standards for what constitutes college and career readiness for students," and 83% agreed that they "assess every student's readiness for college." On average, secondary school teachers rated their schools as excellent or good in preparing students for college.[19]

A Michigan State University (MSU) team ran an online survey in 2011, eliciting twelve thousand responses from teachers in forty states that had adopted the Common Core math standards. Samples were drawn to be representative for each state. Teachers reported that they liked the idea of standards, with 94 percent believing that common standards across states is a good idea; 82 percent reported they had read at least the standards for their own grade. Only 55 percent were aware that their state had formally adopted CCSS; 57 percent viewed Common Core as "somewhat" or "pretty much" the same as their state's former mathematics standards. After being presented with selected standards for their grade, 77 percent thought they were the same as the former standards. Only 38 percent indicated that the lack of textbooks supporting Common Core presented a challenge to implementing the standards.

From one perspective, these data, collected shortly after CCSS's adoption by the states, painted a rosy picture for implementation. It shouldn't be much of a problem, teachers seem to be saying, because not much is changing. But the MSU researchers sounded the alarm. The teachers' amiable response was a huge problem because "the Common Core Math Standards are in fact quite *different* from what has gone on before." The researchers attributed teachers' benign receptiveness to "an ignorance due in part to the traditionally fragmented, incoherent character of the U.S. mathematics curriculum."[20]

Teachers and principals are implementers of reforms: they need to be on board. Recall what Deborah Loewenberg Ball and David K. Cohen said back in the 1990s about standards: "Policies like this one are made in order to change practice, but they can only work through the practice they seek to change. Teachers are at once the targets and the agents of change."[21] That means more than simply gaining endorsements from teachers' unions and administrators' organizations when standards are adopted. Reforms that make teachers' work easier and more effective are more likely to be implemented well than those making it harder and less effective.

Technology illustrates the point. While computers fundamentally altered other occupations, technology advocates spent decades of frustration watching the slow pace at which teachers incorporated computers and other digital tools into classroom routines. Innovators didn't know the best way to use computers with large numbers of children. Effective use was especially difficult for the teachers populating classrooms in the 1980s and 1990s, who were not yet technologically savvy. James Q. Wilson points out that innovations are more likely to take hold when they "facilitate the performance of existing tasks in a way consistent with existing managerial arrangements. Armies did not resist substituting trucks for horse-drawn carts."[22]

Wilson contrasts education reforms that have succeeded with those that have failed: "Education changes have endured when they have not altered the core tasks of the classroom teacher and have faltered or disappeared when they have required a major change in those core tasks."[23] Historians David Tyack and Larry Cuban make a similar point in *Tinkering towards Utopia*.[24] Right from the start, Common Core was recognized as forcing core tasks to change. Here's a typical sentence from press coverage in 2014: "The new Common Core State Standards require students to demonstrate a deeper understanding of math concepts, which means teachers will have to change how they teach those concepts too."[25]

There's an irony here pertaining to technology and CCSS. Today's teachers increasingly turn to their favorite websites to gather curriculum materials, but many of the most popular materials are misaligned with Common Core. Thus, a younger, technologically savvy teaching force is using the internet to gain autonomy over curricular decisions—and weakening the influence of Common Core—when just a couple of decades ago, a lack of sophistication thwarted the technology-based reforms of that era. Moreover, the decentralization of authority that technology encourages suggests that top-down regulation will be even less effective in the future than it has been in the past.

Readers should not take the lessons of this book as evidence of the shibboleth that teachers are inordinately stubborn and resistant to change. It is instead a profession constrained by local organizations (districts, schools, and classrooms), the fundamental nature of clients (students and parents), and a weak body of scientific knowledge supporting its core work (instruction). The last installment of the National Principal and Teacher Survey (formerly the Schools and Staffing Survey), conducted in 2018, revealed that the average teacher possessed about ten years of teaching experience. That means that for at least 40 percent of classroom teachers, the only standards they have ever known professionally are Common Core. They haven't had to unlearn a curricular or instructional regime governed by prior standards. In a few years, a majority of teachers will have worked under no other standards than Common Core.[26]

Principle 5: Future Research Should Focus on the Technical Core of Schooling

Consider the following thought experiment: What if the political and financial backers of Common Core had taken a different path in 2009? What if they had poured resources into discovering new, more powerful ways of teaching and creating new, more effective curricula? After all, the technologies of healthcare look nothing like they did in 1900, when the typical American could look forward to a life expectancy of approximately fifty years. That's compared to a longevity of approximately eighty years today. This remarkable achievement was primarily the product of scientific discoveries, not of setting tougher standards for doctors and hospitals to meet in conducting their work. Medical professions are regulated more closely today than in 1900, of course, but it is hard to imagine what healthcare would be like today without the twentieth century's scientific advancements that gave medical professionals more effective tools for treating patients.

Robert Siegler's research on fractions, mentioned in chapter 4, provides a good example. A fifth grader's knowledge of fractions predicts high school math achievement, even after controlling for student IQ, knowledge of other math topics, and parental education and income.[27]

In a survey conducted for the National Math Advisory Panel in 2007, algebra teachers named word problems and working with fractions as the two areas of weakest preparation for students.[28]

Fractions are like a gigantic wall that kids hit in fourth, fifth, and sixth grades; some crawl over, but many do not. What if the Bill & Melinda Gates Foundation money that went to Common Core, estimated at $300 million, had instead funded dozens of experiments to discover new curricular materials and new ways of teaching fractions, field tested the new programs in randomized trials, and then disseminated the findings broadly?[29] In other words, what if the Gates Foundation had funded science and invention instead of standards and regulation? Notice how these questions begin at the endpoint of standards' intended effects, in core classroom activities, consistent with Elmore's backward mapping.

Future research also must incorporate cost-benefit analysis into policy evaluation. I have not yet seen a comprehensive estimate of Common Core's total cost, but it is easily in the tens of billions of dollars. Future cost-benefit studies of CCSS should also include modeling instructional time as a cost. One aspect of the math standards underscores the importance of time. The activities associated with conceptual understanding—requiring students to present multiple representations, learning and practicing more than one algorithm for arithmetic operations, having students defend their answers either orally or in writing—are not well supported in research as increasing general math achievement. Each of these activities consumes a lot of instructional time. The alternative—presenting a single concrete model, teaching one algorithm for each operation, and keeping writing tasks to a minimum during math lessons—frees up extra instructional time for teachers to spend teaching additional mathematics. There are steep opportunity costs to instructional regimes that linger over concepts in the hope of deepening learning. Time is a precious resource. One of the reasons past math reforms focusing on conceptual understanding have such a dismal history may involve the enormous amount of instructional time that must be devoted to the effort.

A FINAL WORD

Public officials always have had, and surely always will have, an interest in the content of schooling. When standards writing emerged in the late

1980s, state education leaders had already spent much of the twentieth century issuing frameworks, curriculum guides, courses of study, and graduation requirements. Standards are the latest means of regulating the technical core of schooling. In 2020, K–12 public schools will command approximately $750 billion in revenues. A vast bureaucracy is required to channel those billions of dollars where they are needed in the system. It is doubtful that policymakers will soon abandon standards as a strategy for reforming schools. Voters hold them accountable for results. The standards-setting process taps into political skills—satisfying competing interests through log rolling, forging compromises with carefully worded documents—that are second nature to leaders of publicly governed institutions.

But standards give officials at the top of the system only the illusion of control. Writing standards calls on different skills than implementing them. In the end, standards are effective due to influencing the core activities of classrooms, which fall under the sway of teachers. An apt analogy is to a professional sports team, whether in baseball, basketball, football, or hockey. The success of winning teams is often attributed to a savvy owner, a shrewd coach, and several star players. Each has a role to play, but boundaries must be honored. The last thing a successful franchise wants to see is players who think they are coaches or an egomaniacal owner who tries to tell players the best way to play their sport.

The failure of Common Core suggests that the theory of standards-based reform is faulty. Expectations for learning have been frequently unrealistic. Reliable evidence for favoring one instructional approach—or one particular curriculum—over another rarely exists, suggesting that greater efforts at producing scientific breakthroughs should take precedence over more diligent regulation. A new theory is needed that acknowledges the bottom of the education system, where policy may be distant, but real teachers and real students engage in the daily work of teaching and learning.

NOTES

INTRODUCTION

1. US Department of Education Press Office, "Duncan Pushes Back on Attacks on Common Core Standards: Arne Duncan Remarks at the American Society of News Editors Annual Convention, Capitol Hilton, Washington, D.C.," June 25, 2013, https://www.ed.gov/news/speeches/duncan-pushes-back-attacks-common-core -standards.

2. US Senate Committee on Health, Education, Labor, and Pensions, "Alexander: 'The Republican Majority Kept Its Promise to Repeal the Federal Common Core Man-date," press release, February 16, 2016, https://www.help.senate.gov/chair/newsroom /press/alexander-the-republican-majority-kept-its-promise-to-repeal-the-federal -common-core-mandate.

3. Jessica Huseman and Laura Moser, "Trump Says He'd Kill Common Core. No, He Couldn't," *Slate*, February 22, 2016, https://slate.com/human-interest/2016/02 /trump-says-hed-kill-common-core-no-he-couldnt.html.

4. Anya Kamenetz, "DeVos: 'Common Core Is Dead'; A Large Online Charter School is Shut Down," NPR, January 20, 2018, https://www.npr.org/sections/ed/2018/01 /20/578705608/devos-common-core-is-dead-a-large-online-charter-school-is -shut-down.

5. Valerie Strauss, "Florida's New Governor Signs Order to Kill Common Core (though It Was Technically Dead Already)," *Washington Post*, February 1, 2019.

6. Teacher, school, and district numbers are current as of July 2020, using the latest figures from the *Digest of Education Statistics*: teachers, table 208.20; schools, table 216.10; districts, table 214.10.

7. Jeffrey L. Pressman and Aaron Wildavsky, *Implementation: How Great Expec-tations in Washington Are Dashed in Oakland* (Berkeley: University of California Press, 1984). I discuss Pressman and Wildavsky as applied to Common Core in greater detail in Tom Loveless, "Implementing the Common Core: A Look at Cur-riculum," Brookings Institution, May 15, 2014, https://www.brookings.edu/research /implementing-the-common-core-a-look-at-curriculum.

8. Michael Q. McShane, "Navigating the Common Core," AEI, March 18, 2014, https://www.aei.org/articles/navigating-the-common-core/.

9. Tom Loveless, *The Tracking Wars: State Reform Meets School Policy* (Washington, DC: Brookings Institution Press, 1999).

10. Larry Cuban has pointed out limitations of the pendulum metaphor. See Larry Cuban, "Reforming Again, Again, and Again," *Educational Researcher* 19, no. 1 (1990): 3–13.

11. I discuss the CA frameworks in Tom Loveless, "The Use and Misuse of Research in Educational Reform," in *Brookings Papers on Education Policy 1998*, ed. Diane Ravitch (Washington, DC: Brookings Institution), 279–317.

12. Bill Honig, "The California Context, How the California Reading Wars Got Resolved: A Personal Story," Building Better Schools, accessed July 4, 2020, http://www.buildingbetterschools.com/how-the-ca-reading-wars-got-resolved-a-personal-story.

CHAPTER 1

1. Gillard D (2018) *Education in England: a history,* www.educationengland.org.uk/history.

2. *The Royal Commission on the State of Popular Education in England* [Newcastle Report], 1861. Volume I accessed on December 30, 2017, http://www.education england.org.uk/documents/newcastle1861/index.html.

3. Brendan A. Rapple, "Payment by Results: An Example of Assessment in Elementary Education from Nineteenth Century Britain," *Education Policy Analysis Archives* 2, no. 1 (1994): 4.

4. Phoebe Moore, "From Payment by Results to Performance Related Pay" (paper presented at the International Political Economy Group annual conference, Limerick, Ireland, September 13, 2013).

5. Florence S. Boos, "The Education Act of 1870: Before and After," BRANCH: Britain, Representation, and Nineteenth-Century History, accessed May 21, 2020, https://www.branchcollective.org/?ps_articles=florence-s-boos-the-education-act-of-1870-before-and-after.

6. Gillard, "Education in England." Also see Moore, "From Payment by Results to Performance Related Pay," (paper presented at the International Political Economy Group annual conference, Limerick, Ireland, September 13, 2013).

7. Total enrollment in public and private high schools in 1890 was about 5.6% of the age 14–17 population. *Digest of Education Statistics* (Washington, DC: National Center for Education Statistics 2018), table 201.20.

8. William J. Reese, *The Origins of the American High School* (New Haven, CT: Yale University Press, 1995), 209–210.

9. Paul E. Peterson, *The Politics of School Reform, 1870–1940* (Chicago: University of Chicago Press, 1985), 198.

10. Reese, *The Origins of the American High School*, 209–210.

11. Diane Ravitch, *Left Back: A Century of Failed School Reforms* (New York: Simon & Schuster, 2000), 42.

12. Lawrence A. Cremin, *The Transformation of the School: Progressivism in American Education, 1876–1957* (New York: Alfred A. Knopf, 1961), 19.

13. The elementary school curriculum was the explicit focus of the Committee of Fifteen, chaired by Harris. Its report was published in 1895.

14. *Report of the Committee on Secondary School Studies Appointed at the Meeting of the National Educational Association July 9, 1892, with the Reports of the Conferences Arranged by This Committee and Held December 28–30, 1892* (Washington, DC: Government Printing Office, 1893), 143–144.

15. See Cremin, *Transformation of the School*, 276–308.

16. Herbert M. Kliebard, *The Struggle for the American Curriculum, 1893–1958* (New York: Routledge and Kegan Paul, 1987), 23; emphasis in the original.

17. Joseph Mayer Rice, *Scientific Management in Education* (New York: Hinds, Noble, and Eldredge, 1913), 65–81.

18. Rice, 6.

19. Rice, 7.

20. Cremin, *Transformation of the School*, 187

21. David F. Labaree, *The Making of an American High School* (New Haven, CT: Yale University Press, 1988).

22. Daniel P. Resnick, "Minimum Competency Testing Historically Considered," *Review of Research in Education* 8 (1980): 6.

23. Labaree, *Making*, 130.

24. David L. Angus and Jeffrey E. Mirel, *The Failed Promise of the American High School, 1890–1995* (New York: Teachers College Press, 1999), 15.

25. Herbert M. Kliebard, *Changing Course: American Curriculum Reform in the 20th Century* (New York: Teachers College Press, 2002), 47.

26. August William Weber, "State Control of Instruction: A Study of Centralization in Public Education" (PhD diss., University of Wisconsin, 1911), 37.

27. Weber, 61.

28. David Tyack, Thomas James, and Aaron Benavot, *Law and the Shaping of Public Education, 1795–1954* (Madison: University of Wisconsin Press, 1987).

29. James Allan Lufkin, "A History of the California State Textbook Adoption Program" (PhD diss., University of California, Berkeley, 1968).

30. David A. Gamson, Sarah Anne Eckert, and Jeremy Anderson, "Standards, Instructional Objectives, and Curriculum Design: A Complex Relationship," *Phi Delta Kappan* 100, no. 6 (2019): 8–12. Page numbers within the excerpt refer to John Franklin Bobbitt, "Curriculum-Making in Los Angeles," *Supplementary Educational Monographs*, no. 20 (1922).

31. Kliebard, *Changing Course*, 21.

32. Diane Ravitch details Bagley's arguments with progressives in *Left Back*, and a chapter on Bagley is included in J. Wesley Null and Diane Ravitch, eds., *Forgotten Heroes of American Education* (Greenwich, CT: Information Age Publishing, 2006).

33. Kliebard, *Struggle*, 173.

34. William C. Bagley and George C. Kyte, *The California Curriculum Study* (Berkeley: University of California, 1926), 21; italics in the original.

35. Lufkin, "History," 100–110.

36. High school texts were adopted at the district level. See Kenneth K. Wong and Tom Loveless, "The Politics of Textbook Policy: Proposing a Framework," in *Textbooks in American Society*, ed. Philip G. Altbach et al. (Albany: SUNY Press, 1991), 27–41.

37. The legislation allowing the state to lease or to purchase commercial publishers' plates for printing textbooks was passed in 1903 (Lufkin, "History," 86). Beginning

in 1913, Kansas experimented off and on with state printing. See Lewie W. Burnett, "State Textbook Policies, with Particular Reference to State Printing of Textbooks in California," *Phi Delta Kappan* 33, no. 5 (January 1952): 257–261.

38. Irving J. Hendrick, "California's Response to the 'New Education' in the 1930s," *California Historical Quarterly* 53, no. 1 (Spring 1974): 25–40.

39. Ravitch, *Left Back*, 243–244; Hendrick, "California's Response," 36–37.

40. Larry Cuban, *How Teachers Taught: Constancy and Change in American Classrooms, 1890–1990* (New York: Teachers College Press, 1993).

41. Cuban, 82.

42. *Digest of Education Statistics* (Washington, DC: National Center for Education Statistics 2018), table 105.30.

43. Tyack, James, and Benavot, 13–17.

44. Thomas B. Timar, "The Institutional Role of State Education Departments: A Historical Perspective," *American Journal of Education* 105, no. 3 (May 1997): 231–260.

CHAPTER 2

1. Bruno V. Manno, "Remembering 'A Nation at Risk': Reflections on Politics and Policy," *Education Next* (blog), March 22, 2018, https://www.educationnext.org/remembering-nation-risk-reflections-politics-policy/.

2. Tim Sablik, "Recession of 1981–82," *Federal Reserve History*, November 22, 2013, https://www.federalreservehistory.org/essays/recession_of_1981_82.

3. National Commission on Excellence in Education, *A Nation at Risk: The Imperative for Educational Reform* (Washington, DC: US Department of Education, 1983), https://www2.ed.gov/pubs/NatAtRisk/risk.html.

4. David C. Berliner and Bruce J. Biddle, *The Manufactured Crisis: Myths, Fraud, and the Attack on America's Public Schools* (Reading, MA: Addison Wesley, 1995).

5. Diane Ravitch, *Left Back: A Century of Failed School Reforms* (New York: Simon & Schuster, 2000), 412.

6. Ted Bartell and Julie Noble, "Changes in Course Selection by High School Students: The Impact of National Educational Reform," in *The Educational Reform Movement of the 1980s*, ed. Joseph Murphy (Berkeley, CA: McCutchan Publishing Corporation, 1990), 265–276. See also *The 2000 High School Transcript Study Tabulations: Comparative Data on Credits Earned and Demographics for 2000, 1998, 1994, 1990, 1987, and 1982 High School Graduates* (Washington, DC: NCES, 2007).

7. Brian A. Jacob, "Getting Tough? The Impact of High School Graduation Exams," *Educational Evaluation and Policy Analysis* 23, no. 2 (2001): 99–121.

8. Joseph Murphy, ed., *The Educational Reform Movement of the 1980s* (Berkeley, CA: McCutchan Publishing Corporation, 1990), 6.

9. Peter W. Airasian, "State Mandated Testing and Educational Reform: Context and Consequences," *American Journal of Education* 95, no. 3 (1987): 393–412; George M. Madaus, "The Influence of Testing on the Curriculum," in *Critical Issues in Curriculum: Eighty-Seventh Yearbook of the National Society for the Study of Education*, ed. Laurel N. Tanner (Chicago: University of Chicago Press, 1988), 83–121.

10. Tom Loveless, "Why Standards Produce Weak Reform," in *Bush-Obama School Reform: Lessons Learned*, ed. Frederick M. Hess and Michael Q. McShane (Cambridge, MA: Harvard Education Press, 2018), 107–124.

11. Marshall S. Smith and Jennifer A. O'Day, "Systemic School Reform," in *The Politics of Curriculum and Testing*, ed. Susan H. Fuhrman and Betty Malen (London, England: Taylor & Francis, 1990), 233–267.

12. Jennifer A. O'Day and Marshall S. Smith, "Systemic Reform and Educational Opportunity," in *Designing Coherent Education Policy*, ed. Susan H. Fuhrman (San Francisco: Jossey-Bass Publishers, 1993), 250–312.

13. Smith and O'Day, 233–267.

14. Smith and O'Day, 239.

15. David K. Cohen and Deborah Loewenberg Ball, "Policy and Practice: An Overview," *Educational Evaluation and Policy Analysis* 13, no. 3 (Fall 1990): 233–239.

16. Cohen and Ball, 237.

17. Diane Ravitch, *National Standards in Education: A Citizen's Guide* (Washington, DC: Brookings Institution, 1995). Also see Tom Loveless, "Why Standards Produce Weak Reform," in *Bush-Obama School Reform: Lessons Learned*, ed. Frederick M. Hess and Michael Q. McShane (Cambridge, MA: Harvard Education Press, 2018), 107–124.

18. Lynne V. Cheney, "The End of History," *Wall Street Journal*, October 20, 1994, A22.

19. Loveless, "Weak Reform," 109.

20. The first of the antimath reform websites was titled Mathematically Correct. The site is no longer maintained, but it is archived at https://web.archive.org/web /20111128152658/http://www.mathematicallycorrect.com. The second was NYC HOLD, and it is archived at https://web.archive.org/web/20111224110454/http:// www.nychold.com/.

21. Steven Leinwand, "It's Time to Abandon Computational Algorithms," *Education Week*, February 9, 1994, https://www.edweek.org/ew/articles/1994/02/09/20lein .h13.html/.

22. John R. Anderson, Lynne M. Reder, and Herbert A. Simon, "Radical Constructivism and Cognitive Psychology," in *Brookings Papers on Education Policy 1998*, ed. Diane Ravitch (Washington, DC: Brookings Institution, 1998), 227–278.

23. Education Week, *Quality Counts 1999: Rewarding Results, Punishing Failure* (Bethesda, MD: Editorial Projects in Education, 1999).

24. Patrick J. McGuinn, *No Child Left Behind and the Transformation of Federal Education Policy, 1965–2005* (Lawrence: University Press of Kansas, 2006), 182.

25. Margaret E. Goertz and Mark C. Duffy, *Assessment and Accountability Systems in the 50 States: 1999–2000* (Philadelphia: CPRE Research Reports, 2001).

26. Martin Carnoy and Susanna Loeb, "Does External Accountability Affect Student Outcomes? A Cross-State Analysis," *Educational Evaluation and Policy Analysis* 24, no. 4 (December 2002): 305–331.

27. Eric A. Hanushek and Margaret E. Raymond, "Does School Accountability Lead to Improved Student Performance?," *Journal of Policy Analysis and Management* 24, no. 2 (Spring 2005): 297–327.

28. Audrey L. Amrein and David C. Berliner, "High-Stakes Testing and Student Learning," *Education Policy Analysis Archives* 10, no. 18 (March 2002), https://doi.org /10.14507/epaa.v10n18.2002.

29. Peter Schmidt, "Baltimore Resists Order to 'Reconstitute' 3 Schools," *Education Week*, February 15, 1995, https://www.edweek.org/ew/articles/1995/02/15/21balt. h14.html; Millicent Lawton, "California Districts Fighting State Testing Orders,"

Education Week, March 4, 1998, https://www.edweek.org/ew/articles/1998/03
/04/25test.h17.html; Debra Viadero and Julie Blair, "Error Affects Test Results in
Six States," *Education Week*, September 29, 1999, 1, 13–15, https://www.edweek
.org/ew/articles/1999/09/29/05ctb.h19.html.

30. Deborah Meier, "Educating a Democracy," in *Will Standards Save Public Education?*, ed. Joshua Cohen and Joel Rogers (Boston: Beacon Press, 2000): 3–31. Also
see Nicholas Tampio, Common Core: *National Education Standards and the Threat
to Democracy* (Baltimore: Johns Hopkins University Press, 2018).

31. Drew Lindsay, "CON-Test," *Education Week*, April 5, 2000, 30–37.

32. Kerry A. White, "Student Protesters in Massachusetts Sit Out State Exam," *Education Week*, June 2, 1999, 14–15.

33. Lynn Olson, "An 'A' or a 'D': State Rankings Differ Widely," *Education Week*, April
15, 1998, https://www.edweek.org/ew/articles/1998/04/15/31stand.h17.html.

34. In addition, 95% of students were required to take the state's annual test.

35. Frederick M. Hess, "Accountability without Angst? Public Opinion and No Child
Left Behind," AEI, December 29, 2006, https://www.aei.org/articles/accountability
-without-angst-public-opinion-and-no-child-left-behind/.

36. Thomas B. Timar, "The Institutional Role of State Education Departments: A Historical Perspective," *American Journal of Education* 105, no. 3 (May 1997): 244.

37. Milbrey W. McLaughlin and Lorrie A. Shephard, *Improving Education through
Standards-Based Reform: A Report by the National Academy of Education Panel on
Standards-based Education Reform* (Stanford, CA: National Academy of Education,
1995), 26.

38. Paul Berman and Milbrey W. McLaughlin, *Federal Programs Supporting Educational Change: Vol. VIII, Implementing and Sustaining Innovations* (Santa Monica,
CA: RAND Corporation, 1978).

39. Richard F. Elmore, "Complexity and Control: What Legislators and Administrators
Can Do about Implementing Policy," in *Handbook of Teaching and Policy*, ed. Lee S.
Shulman and Gary Sykes (New York: Longman, 1983), 342–369.

CHAPTER 3

1. Naomi Chudowsky and Vic Chudowsky, *Many States Have Taken a "Backloaded
Approach" to No Child Left Behind Goal of All Students Scoring "Proficient"* (Washington, DC: Center on Education Policy, 2008).

2. For a list of student protests, see Tom Loveless, "Test Based Accountability: The
Promise and the Perils," in *Brookings Papers on Education Policy 2005*, ed. Diane
Ravitch (Washington, DC: Brookings Institution), 7–45.

3. Thomas S. Dee and Brian A. Jacob, "Evaluating NCLB," *Education Next* 10, no. 3
(Summer 2010): 54–61. For a more technically oriented version of the paper, see
Thomas S. Dee and Brian A. Jacob, "The Impact of No Child Left Behind on Student Achievement," *Journal of Policy Analysis and Management* 30, no. 3 (Summer
2011): 418–446.

4. Manyee Wong, Thomas D. Cook, and Peter M. Steiner, "Adding Design Elements
to Improve Time Series Designs: No Child Left Behind as an Example of Causal
Pattern Matching," *Journal of Research on Educational Effectiveness* 8, no. 2 (2015):
245–279, https://doi.org/10.1080/19345747.2013.878011.

5. Paul E. Peterson and Frederick M. Hess, "Keeping an Eye on State Standards: A Race to the Bottom?," *Education Next* 6, no. 3 (Summer 2006): 28.

6. Sam Dillon, "Federal Researchers Find Lower Standards in Schools," *New York Times,* October 30, 2009.

7. William Harms, "Immediate Rewards for Good Scores Can Boost Student Performance," *UChicago News,* June 26, 2012, https://news.uchicago.edu/story/immediate -rewards-good-scores-can-boost-student-performance/.

8. Uri Gneezy et al., *Measuring Success in Education: The Role of Effort on the Test Itself,* working paper 24004 (Cambridge, MA: National Bureau of Economic Research).

9. US General Accounting Office, *Educational Achievement Standards: NAGB's Approach Yields Misleading Interpretations* (Washington, DC: US General Accounting Office, June 1993); National Research Council, *Grading the Nation's Report Card: Evaluating NAEP and Transforming the Assessment of Educational Progress* (Washington, DC: National Academies Press, 1999), https://doi.org/10.17226/6296; Lorrie Shepard et al., *Setting Performance Standards for Student Achievement: A Report of the NAE Panel on the Evaluation of the NAEP Trial State Assessment: An Evaluation of the 1992 Achievement Levels* (Stanford, CA: National Academy of Education, 1993).

10. For a fuller discussion of NAEP's performance levels, see: Tom Loveless, "The NAEP Proficiency Myth," Brookings Institution, June 13, 2016, https://www .brookings.edu/blog/brown-center-chalkboard/2016/06/13/the-naep-proficiency -myth/.

11. Leslie A. Scott and Steven J. Ingels, *Interpreting 12th-Graders' NAEP-Scaled Mathematics Performance Using High School Predictors and Postsecondary Outcomes from the National Education Longitudinal Study of 1988 (NELS:88)* (Washington, DC: National Center for Education Statistics, 2007), NCES 2007-328. See page vii of the Executive Summary.

12. Clifford Adelman, *The Toolbox Revisited: Paths to Degree Completion from High School through College* (Washington, DC: Office of Vocational and Adult Education, US Department of Education, 2006).

13. Abigail Hess, "The 10 Most Educated Countries in the World," CNBC, February 7, 2018, https://www.cnbc.com/2018/02/07/the-10-most-educated-countries-in-the -world.html.

14. United States Census Bureau, "Highest Educational Levels Reached by Adults in the U.S. since 1940," US Census Bureau, press release CB17-51, March 30, 2017, https://www.census.gov/newsroom/press-releases/2017/cb17-51.html.

15. Andrew Trotter, "Poll Finds Rise in Unfavorable Views of NCLB," *Education Week,* August 27, 2007.

16. Al Behrman, "An Unlikely Partnership Left Behind," *Washington Post,* April 11, 2007.

17. Caitlin Scott, *A Call to Restructure Restructuring* (Washington, DC: Center on Education Policy, 2008).

18. National Governors Association, Council of Chief State School Officers, and Achieve, Inc., *Benchmarking for Success: Ensuring U.S. Students Receive a World-Class Education* (Washington, DC: National Governors Association, 2008).

19. *Benchmarking for Success,* 24.

20. Robert Rothman, *Something in Common: The Common Core Standards and the Next Chapter in American Education* (Cambridge, MA: Harvard Education Press, 2011); Robert Rothman, *Fewer, Clearer, Higher: How the Common Core State Standards Can Change Classroom Practice* (Cambridge, MA: Harvard Education Press, 2013).

21. Lyndsey Layton, "How Bill Gates Pulled Off the Swift Common Core Revolution," *Washington Post*, June 7, 2014, https://www.washingtonpost.com/politics/how-bill-gates-pulled-off-the-swift-common-core-revolution/2014/06/07/a830e32e-ec34-11e3-9f5c-9075d5508f0a_story.html.

22. Mercedes K. Schneider, Common Core Dilemma: Who Owns Our Schools? (New York: Teachers College Press, 2015).

23. Rothman, *Something in Common*, 63–82.

24. Schneider, *Common Core Dilemma*, 104.

25. Schneider, *Common Core Dilemma*, 81

26. Rothman, *Fewer, Clearer, Higher*, 7.

27. Sean Cavanaugh, "Openness of Common-Standards Process at Issue," *Education Week*, August 11, 2009, https://www.edweek.org/ew/articles/2009/08/12/37standardsprocess-2.h28.html.

28. Catherine Gewertz, "Comments Pouring in on Common Standards, but You Won't See Them," *Education Week*, March 22, 2010, https://blogs.edweek.org/edweek/curriculum/2010/03/comments_pouring_in_on_common.html.

29. Rick Hess, "Common-Core Validation Committee Non-Signer Dylan Wiliam Shares a Couple Thoughts," *Education Week*, September 15, 2014, https://blogs.edweek.org/edweek/rick_hess_straight_up/2014/09/common_core_validation_committee_non-signer_dylan_wiliam_shares_thoughts.html.

30. Sandra Stotsky, "Invalid Process of Common Core Development" (presentation, American Principles Project, South Bend, IN, September 2013), https://www.youtube.com/watch?v=TuHGhQJDre4/. Also see Schneider, *Common Core Dilemma*, 77–81

31. Arne Duncan, "States Will Lead the Way Towards Reform," (speech, 2009 Governors Education Symposium, Cary, NC, June 14, 2009); see https://www.ed.gov/news/speeches/states-will-lead-way-toward-reform.

32. Rothman, *Something in Common*, 104.

33. Rothman, *Fewer, Clearer, Higher*, 9.

34. Stotsky did not attend the board meeting approving CCSS because of an injury. See Stephen Sawchuk, "Mass. Adopts Common Standards amidst Fiery Debate," *Education Week*, July 21, 2010, https://www.edweek.org/ew/articles/2010/07/21/39massachusetts.h29.html.

35. "State Approves New Common Core Educational Standards," *Los Angeles Daily News*, August 2, 2010, https://www.dailynews.com/2010/08/02/state-approves-new-common-core-educational-standards/.

36. Michael Newman, "American Public Ready for National Curriculum, Achievement Standards, Annual Gallup Poll Finds," *Education Week*, September 6, 1989, https://www.edweek.org/ew/articles/1989/09/06/09020017.h09.html.

37. John W. Kingdon, *Agendas, Alternatives, and Public Policies* (New York: HarperCollins, 1984).

38. Achieve, "Strong Support, Low Awareness: Public Perception of the Common Core State Standards," Achieve, October 1, 2011, https://www.achieve.org/publications /strong-support-low-awareness-public-perception-common-core-state-standards. (Note that Achieve shut down on December 31, 2020, but indicated that its intellectual property would be made publicly available.)

39. Schneider, *Common Core Dilemma*, 157.

40. Sean Cavanaugh, "Republicans Gain Clout in State-Level Offices," *Education Week*, November 3, 2010.

41. William G. Howell, Martin R. West, and Paul E. Peterson, "The Public Weighs in on School Reform," *Education Next* 11, no. 4 (Fall 2011), https://www.educationnext .org/the-public-weighs-in-on-school-reform/.

CHAPTER 4

1. Math educators routinely use the singular term *number* to refer to the learning domain that includes number sense.

2. The 1996 NAEP Framework for math declared its intention to "move NAEP assessments ever closer to the vision embodied in the NCTM curriculum *Standards*." *Mathematics Framework for the 1996 National Assessment of Educational Progress* (Washington, DC: College Board, 1996), 14. On the influence of the NCTM standards on state standards, see Ralph A. Raimi and Lawrence Braden, *State Math Standards* (Washington, DC: Thomas B. Fordham Foundation, 1998).

3. Anne Turnbaugh Lockwood, *Conversations with Educational Leaders: Contemporary Viewpoints on Education* (Albany: SUNY Press, 1997), 197.

4. Raimi and Braden, *State Math Standards*, 10; italics in original.

5. Robert Siegler et al., "Early Predictors of High School Mathematics Achievement," *Psychological Science* 21, no. 7 (2012).

6. See http://www.corestandards.org/Math/Content/3/NF/

7. See http://www.corestandards.org/Math/Content/3/NF/

8. See http://www.corestandards.org/Math/Content/3/NF/.

9. See http://www.corestandards.org/Math/Content/3/NF/.

10. See http://www.corestandards.org/Math/Content/3/NF.

11. See http://www.corestandards.org/Math/Content/3/NF.

12. See http://www.corestandards.org/Math/Content/3/NF.

13. See http://www.corestandards.org/Math/Content/3/NF.

14. See http://www.corestandards.org/Math/Content/3/NF.

15. See Edward Frenkel and Hung-His Wu, "Republicans Should Love 'Common Core,'" *Wall Street Journal*, May 6, 2013. For reporting on the fractions in the math standards, see Liana Heitlin, "Approach to Fractions Seen as Key Shift in Common Standards," *Education Week*, November 10, 2014, https://www.edweek.org/ew /articles/2014/11/12/12cc-fractions.h34.html.

16. Tom Loveless, "Common Core and Classroom Instruction: The Good, the Bad, and the Ugly," Education Next, last updated May 19, 2015, https://www.educationnext .org/common-core-classroom-instruction-good-bad-ugly/.

17. See http://www.corestandards.org/ELA-Literacy/W/6/1/.

18. See http://www.corestandards.org/ELA-Literacy/W/6/1/.

19. See http://www.corestandards.org/ELA-Literacy/W/6/1/.

20. See http://www.corestandards.org/ELA-Literacy/W/6/1/.

21. See http://www.corestandards.org/ELA-Literacy/W/6/1/.

22. See http://www.corestandards.org/ELA-Literacy/W/6/1/.

23. Richard F. Elmore, "Backward Mapping: Implementation Research and Policy Decisions," *Political Science Quarterly* 94, no. 4 (Winter 1979–1980): 604.

24. *Common Core State Standards for English Language Arts & Literacy in History/Social Studies, Science, and Technical Subjects* (Washington, DC: Common Core State Standards Initiative, 2010).

25. *Standards for ELA*, 11.

26. See, for example, Robert Rothman, *Something in Common: The Common Core Standards and the Next Chapter in American Education* (Cambridge, MA: Harvard Education Press, 2011), 84.

27. *Standards for ELA*, 6.

28. Louisa Moats, "When Will We Ever Learn? The Common Core State Standards with Dr. Louisa Moats," *Psychology Today*, (blog) January 21, 2014.

29. Louisa Moats, "Reconciling Common Core with Reading Research," *Perspectives on Language and Literacy* 38, no. 4 (Fall 2012): 2.

30. *Standards for ELA*, appendix A, 7.

31. Lynn D. Fielding, Jay Maidment, and Christian N. K. Anderson, *Readiness for Entering Kindergarten: The Impact on Future Academic Achievement* (Kennewick, WA: Children's Reading Foundation, 2019), 2.

32. *Common Core State Standards for Mathematics* (Washington, DC: Common Core State Standards Initiative, 2010), 5.

33. Blended learning at the secondary level also typically involves students watching teachers' lectures or other forms of direct instruction at home so that classroom time can be devoted to class discussion or one-on-one interactions. That component does not appear to have been part of the Teach to One program in Elizabeth.

34. Douglas Ready et al., *Final Impact Results from the i3 Implementation of Teach to One: Math.* (New York: Consortium for Policy Research in Education at Teachers College, Columbia University, 2019).

35. Ready et al., 18–19

36. See Jay Mathews, "Fiction vs. Nonfiction Smackdown," *Washington Post*, October 17, 2012, http://www.washingtonpost.com/local/education/fiction-vs-nonfiction-smackdown/2012/10/17/cbb333d0-16f0-11e2-a55c-39408fbe6a4b_story.html.

37. Daniel Willingham, "School Time, Knowledge, and Reading Comprehension," *Daniel Willingham—Science & Education* (blog), March 7, 2012, http://www.danielwillingham.com/daniel-willingham-science-and-education-blog/school-time-knowledge-and-reading-comprehension.

38. Donna R. Recht and Lauren Leslie, "Effect of Prior Knowledge on Good and Poor Readers' Memory of Text," *Journal of Educational Psychology* 80, no. 1 (1988): 16–20.

39. Catherine Gewertz, "Tackling the Fiction/Nonfiction Balance in the Common Core (Again)," *Education Week*, February 1, 2013, https://blogs.edweek.org/edweek/curriculum/2013/02/fiction_and_nonfiction_common.html.

40. Mark Bauerlein and Sandra Stotsky, *How Common Core's ELA Standards Place College Readiness at Risk* (Boston: Pioneer Institute, 2012).

41. The Gettysburg Unit is available at https://www.engageny.org/resource/common-core-exemplar-for-high-school-ela-lincoln-s-gettysburg-address.

42. I first made the observations in this paragraph in a blog post: Tom Loveless, "Implementing Common Core: Curriculum Part 3," Brookings Institution, October 9, 2014, https://www.brookings.edu/research/implementing-common-core-curriculum -part-3/.

43. See "Key Shifts in Mathematics," Common Core State Standards Initiative, accessed September 30, 2020, http://www.corestandards.org/other-resources/key-shifts-in -mathematics/.

44. Richard Askey presents several cases of bad mathematics in reform texts: Richard Askey, "Good Intentions Are Not Enough," in *The Great Curriculum Debate*, ed. Tom Loveless (Washington, DC: Brookings Institution Press, 2001), 163–183.

45. Jo Boaler, "Timed Tests and the Development of Math Anxiety," *Education Week*, July 3, 2012.

46. Jo Boaler, "Fluency without Fear: Research Evidence on the Best Ways to Learn Math Facts," youcubed, January 28, 2015, https://www.youcubed.org/evidence /fluency-without-fear/.

47. Jo Boaler, "Fluency without Fear: Research Evidence on the Best Ways to Learn Math Facts," youcubed, January 28, 2015, https://www.youcubed.org/evidence /fluency-without-fear/.

48. Paul A. Kirschner, John Sweller, and Richard E. Clark, "Why Minimal Guidance during Instruction Does Not Work: And Analysis of the Failure of Constructivist, Discovery, Problem-Based, Experiential, and Inquiry-Based Teaching," *Educational Psychologist* 41, no. 2 (2006): 75–86.

49. Jason Zimba, "Can Parents Help with Math Homework? YES," Thomas B. Fordham Institute, January 15, 2016, https://fordhaminstitute.org/national/commentary/can -parents-help-math-homework-yes/.

50. Amber M. Northern, "Does Common Core Math Expect Memorization? A Candid Conversation with Jason Zimba," Thomas B. Fordham Institute, July 13, 2016, https://fordhaminstitute.org/national/commentary/does-common-core-math -expect-memorization-candid-conversation-jason-zimba/.

51. Northern, "A Conversation."

CHAPTER 5

1. William J. Bushaw and Shane J. Lopez, "Which Way Do We Go?," *Phi Delta Kappan* 95, no. 1 (2013): 9–25. Of respondents who had heard of CCSS, 28% said they were not very knowledgeable and 6% said they were not at all knowledgeable.

2. Frederick M. Hess, "How the Common Core Went Wrong," *National Affairs*, no. 45, Fall 2014, 3–19, https://www.nationalaffairs.com/publications/detail/how-the -common-core-went-wrong.

3. *Joint Statement of Early Childhood Health and Education Professionals on the Common Core Standards Initiative* (Annapolis: Alliance for Childhood. 2010).

4. Meisels's critique is in Valerie Strauss, "Common Core Standards Pose Dilemma for Early Childhood," *Washington Post*, November 29, 2011; Yatvin's critique is in Valerie Strauss, "Choking on the Common Core Standards," *Washington Post*, December 4, 2011.

5. Diane Ravitch, "My View of the Common Core Standards," *Diane Ravitch's Blog*, July 9, 2012, https://dianeravitch.net/2012/07/09/my-view-of-the-common-core -standards/.

6. Ravitch, "My View."

7. Andrew Ujifusa, "Indiana State Schools Chief Loses in Upset," *Education Week*, November 13, 2012, https://www.edweek.org/ew/articles/2012/11/14/12elect-indiana.h32.html/.

8. Stephanie Simon, "Common Core: Business vs. Tea Party," *Politico*, March 14, 2014.

9. Tom Loveless, "Predicting the Effect of the Common Core State Standards," in *The 2012 Brown Center Report on American Education* (Washington, DC: Brookings Institution, 2012), 6–14.

10. For a video of Schmidt's presentation, see William H. Schmidt, "Common Core Math Standards Implementation Can Lead to Improved Student Achievement," presentation to the National Press Club, Washington, DC, May 3, 2012, https://www.youtube.com/watch?v=WQ7iWGwTIYQ.

11. William H. Schmidt and Richard T. Houang, "Curricular Coherence and the Common Core State Standards for Mathematics," *Educational Researcher* 41, no. 8 (2012): 294–308.

12. Ze'ev Wurman, "Why Common Core's Math Standards Don't Measure Up," Pioneer Institute, June 24, 2013, https://pioneerinstitute.org/news/why-common-cores-math-standards-dont-measure-up-by-guest-blogger-zeev-wurman/.

13. Tom Loveless, "A Progress Report on Common Core," in *The 2014 Brown Center Report on American Education* (Washington, DC: Brookings Institution, 2014). Schmidt and Houang's congruence rating has a range of 662 to 826, a mean of 762, and an SD of 33.5. From the regression, the coefficient for the congruence rating was 0.08.

14. Catherine Gewertz, "Common-Core Curricula Spark Teacher Resistance," *Education Week*, March 26, 2013, https://www.edweek.org/ew/articles/2013/03/27/26newyork_ep.h32.html.

15. "The Pineapple and the Hare: Pearson's Absurd, Nonsensical ELA Exam, Recycled Endlessly throughout Country," *NYC Public School Parents* (blog), April 19, 2012, https://nycpublicschoolparents.blogspot.com/2012/04/pineapple-and-hare-pearsons-absurd.html.

16. Javier C. Hernández and Robert Gebeloff, "Test Scores Sink as New York Adopts Tougher Benchmarks," *New York Times*, August 7, 2013, https://www.nytimes.com/2013/08/08/nyregion/under-new-standards-students-see-sharp-decline-in-test-scores.html.

17. NY Senate Republicans, "Senator Griffo's Education Town Hall with NYS Education Commissioner D. John King Jr.," YouTube, October 8, 2013, https://youtu.be/2ymjQcFP8sU.

18. CBS6 Albany, "State Ed Commissioner Talks Common Core Controversy," YouTube, October 30, 2013, https://www.youtube.com/watch?v=8eonpSrklmY.

19. Peter DeWitt, "New Forums Scheduled, but N.Y. State Commissioner Pressured to Step Down," *Education Week*, October 26, 2013, https://blogs.edweek.org/edweek/finding_common_ground/2013/10/new_forums_scheduled_but_ny_state_commissioner_pressured_to_step_down.html.

20. Jaime Franchi, "LI Parents & Teachers Revolt against Common Core," *Long Island Press*, November 29, 2013, https://www.longislandpress.com/2013/11/29/li-parents-teachers-revolt-against-common-core/.

21. Michele McNeil, "AYP Glass Half Full for States," *Education Week,* January 10, 2012, https://www.edweek.org/ew/articles/2012/01/11/15cep.h31.html.

22. Morgan S. Polikoff et al., "The Waive of the Future? School Accountability in the Waiver Era," *Educational Researcher* 43, no. 1 (January 2014): 45–54.

23. Patrick McGuinn, "Incentives and Inducement: The Feds Fight Federalism," in *Bush-Obama School Reform: Lessons Learned,* ed. Frederick M. Hess and Michael Q. McShane (Cambridge, MA: Harvard Education Press, 2018), 51–68.

24. Michael J. Petrilli, "If You Support Common Core, Oppose Arne Duncan's 'Waivers,'" Thomas B. Fordham Institute, August 10, 2011, https://fordhaminstitute .org/ohio/commentary/if-you-support-common-core-oppose-arne-duncans -waivers.

25. Eyder Peralta, "Indiana Becomes First State to Back Out of Common Core," NPR, March 24, 2014, https://www.npr.org/sections/thetwo-way/2014/03/24/293894857 /indiana-becomes-first-state-to-back-out-of-common-core.

26. Andrew Ujifusa, "S.C. Governor Signs Bills Requiring State to Replace Common Core," *Education Week,* June 4, 2014, http://blogs.edweek.org/edweek/state _edwatch/2014/06/south_carolina_gov_haley_signs_bill_to.html.

27. Caitlin Emma, "Fallin Signs Common Core Repeal Bill," *Politico*, June 5, 2014, https://www.politico.com/story/2014/06/common-core-repeal-oklahoma-mary -fallin-107499.

28. Lindsey Layton, "Legislatures Taking State Education into Their Own Hands," *Washington Post*, August 2, 2014.

29. Layton, "Legislatures."

30. Keith Ridler, "Lawmakers Consider Fate of Idaho's Common Core Standards," IdahoNews, January 15, 2020, https://idahonews.com/news/local/lawmakers-consider -fate-of-idahos-common-core-standards.

31. Megan Reposa, "South Dakota Replaced Common Core, but Did It Really?," *Argus Leader*, March 14, 2018, https://www.argusleader.com/story/news/education /2018/03/24/south-dakota-replaced-common-core-but-did-really/451123002/.

32. Matt Barnum, "Maine Went All In on 'Proficiency-Based Learning'—then Rolled It Back," Chalkbeat, October 18, 2018, https://www.chalkbeat.org/2018/10/18/21105950 /maine-went-all-in-on-proficiency-based-learning-then-rolled-it-back-what-does -that-mean-for-the-rest.

33. Chelsea Davis, "Montana Smarter Balanced Test Results Improve Slightly, Ditch Glitches of 2015," *Missoulian,* August 17, 2016, https://missoulian.com/news/local /montana-smarter-balanced-test-results-improve-slightly-ditch-glitches-of/article _4989c40c-17cc-5fab-b483-20ea219a1177.html.

34. Andrew Ujifusa, "Nevada Escapes Federal Penalty after 2015 Smarter Balanced Testing Glitches," EdWeek Market Brief, March 17, 2016, https://marketbrief .edweek.org/marketplace-k-12/14115/.

35. Andrew Ujifusa, "Vendors at Odds over Nevada Testing Problems," *Education Week*, May 6, 2015.

36. Matt Barnum, "Arne Duncan's Wrong Turn on Reform: How Federal Dollars Fueled the Testing Backlash," The 74, July 22, 2015, https://www.the74million.org /article/arne-duncans-wrong-turn-on-reform-how-federal-dollars-fueled-the -testing-backlash/.

37. Elizabeth A. Harris, "As Common Core Tests Are Ushered In, Parents and Students Opt Out," *New York Times*, March 1, 2015.
38. Alyson Klein, "Ed. Dept. to States: Even Under ESSA, You Need a Plan for High Opt-Out Rates," *Education Week*, December 22, 2015, http://blogs.edweek.org /edweek/campaign-k-12/2015/12/ed_dept_to_states_under_essa_need_plan_for _opt-Outs.html.
39. Michelle Croft and Richard Lee, *State Legislatures Opting In to Opting Out* (ACT Research & Policy, Issue Brief, 2016).
40. Matthew M. Chingos, "Who Opts Out of State Tests?," Brookings Institution, June 18, 2015, https://www.brookings.edu/research/who-opts-out-of-state-tests/. See also Monte Whaley, "Colorado PARCC Tests Show Concerns in Opt-Outs, Small Gains in Second Year of Scores," *Denver Post*, August 11, 2016, https://www .denverpost.com/2016/08/11/colorado-standardized-tests-small-gains-opt-outs/.
41. Joie Tyrrell and Michael R. Ebert, "Survey: 47 Percent Opted Out of State ELA Exam," *Newsday*, April 12, 2019.
42. Jonathan Supovitz, Alan Daly, and Miguel del Fresno, *#commoncore Project, 2017*, https://www.hashtagcommoncore.com/.
43. Supovitz, Daly, and del Fresno, PDF version, 33.
44. Barnum, "Duncan's Wrong Turn."
45. Lindsey Layton, "Even as Congress Moves to Strip His Power, Arne Duncan Holds His Ground," *Washington Post*, July 8, 2015, https://www.washingtonpost.com /local/education/as-congress-moves-to-strip-his-power-duncan-is-staying-until -the-final-buzzer/2015/07/08/cb0c9d28-15d4-11e5-9ddc-e3353542100c_story.html.
46. Tom LoBianco, "Common Core Attacks All the Rage for Trump, Republicans," CNN, January 28, 2016, https://www.cnn.com/2016/01/28/politics/common-core -donald-trump/index.html.
47. "Louis C K on Letterman May 1, 2014, Common Core Standardized Testing," YouTube, May 2, 2014, https://www.youtube.com/watch?v=HZbd7qEG3Ns.
48. Charles Roberts, "Student's Response to Math Problem Goes Viral, Sparks Debate (Photo)," Opposing Views, March 6, 2018, https://www.opposingviews.com /category/students-response-math-problem-goes-viral-sparks-debate-photo.
49. Christine Rousselle, "Common Core Math Is Ridiculous," Townhall, October 4, 2013, https://townhall.com/tipsheet/christinerousselle/2013/10/04/common -core-math-is-ridiculous-n1717049. The question can be viewed at https://www .pinterest.com/pin/266134659207622532/.
50. Liana Heitin Loewus, "Reactions to the 'Common Core' Math Problem That Went
51. Viral," *Education Week*, April 21, 2014, https://www.edweek.org/teaching-learning /reactions-to-the-common-core-math-problem-that-went-viral/2014/04.
52. Sarah Garland, "Why Is This Common Core Math Problem So Hard?," *Hechinger Report*, March 26, 2014.
53. Item number 10 on this webpage: "18 Times Kids Proved Themselves to Be Miniature Geniuses," *Daily Edge*, November 4, 2015, https://www.dailyedge.ie/kids-are -so-damn-smart-2425513-Nov2015/.
54. "18 Times," item number 1.
55. Andrew Ujifusa, "Pledging a Do-Over on Common Core, N.Y. Gov. Cuomo Announces New Task Force," *Education Week*, September 29, 2015, http://blogs

.edweek.org/edweek/state_edwatch/2015/09/pledging_a_do-over_on_common
_core_ny_gov_cuomo_announces_new_task_force.html.

56. Patrick McGuinn and Jonathan A. Supovitz, *Parallel Play in the Education Sandbox: The Common Core and the Politics of Transpartisan Coalitions* (CPRE Research Reports, 2016), http://repository.upenn.edu/cpre_researchreports/85.

57. Lorraine McDonnel and M. Stephen Weatherford, "Organized Interests and the Common Core," *Educational Researcher* 42, no. 9 (2013): 488–497.

CHAPTER 6

1. Joshua D. Angrist and Jörn-Steffen Pischke, *Mastering Metrics: The Path from Cause to Effect* (Princeton, NJ: Princeton University Press, 2014). One key assumption of differences in differences is that unobserved influences remain fixed. See chapter 4 for illustrations of regression discontinuity designs and chapter 5 for differences in differences, along with discussions of key assumptions of both strategies.

2. For a discussion of differences in differences as applied to international education, see Jan-Eric Gustafsson, "Understanding Causal Influences on Educational Achievement through Analysis of Differences over Time within Countries," in *Lessons Learned*, ed. Tom Loveless (Washington, DC: Brookings Institution, 2007), 37–64.

3. Mengli Song, Rui Yang, and Michael Garet, *Effects of States' Adoption of College- and Career-Ready Standards on Student Achievement*, accessed August 11, 2019, https://www.c-sail.org/publications/effects-states%E2%80%99-adoption-college-and-career-ready-standards-student-achievement.

4. Matt Barnum, "Nearly a Decade Later, Did the Common Core Work? New Research Offers Clues," Chalkbeat, April 29, 2019, https://www.chalkbeat.org/2019/4/29/21121004/nearly-a-decade-later-did-the-common-core-work-new-research-offers-clues. Mengli Song, "Song: Did Common Core Standards Work? New Study Finds Small but Disturbing Negative Impacts on Students' Academic Achievement," The 74, June 4, 2019, https://www.the74million.org/article/song-did-common-core-standards-work-new-study-finds-small-but-disturbing-negative-impacts-on-students-academic-achievement/.

5. Thomas S. Dee and Brian A. Jacob, "Evaluating NCLB," *Education Next* 10, no. 3 (Summer 2010): 54–61; Manyee Wong, Thomas D. Cook, and Peter M. Steiner, "Adding Design Elements to Improve Time Series Designs: No Child Left Behind as an Example of Causal Pattern Matching," *Journal of Research on Educational Effectiveness* 8, no. 2 (2015): 245–279, https://doi.org/10.1080/19345747.2013.878011.

6. Rick Hess and Adam Edgerton, "The Elusive Goldilocks Model of School Reform," Center on Standards, Alignment, Instruction, and Learning, December 7, 2017, https://www.c-sail.org/resources/blog/elusive-goldilocks-model-school-reform.

7. Virginia is included in the ELA analysis because it adopted ELA standards in 2010.

8. The first two NAEP testing years are omitted to address multicollinearity.

9. Kathleen Kennedy Manzo, "Florida Legislators Want Rewrite of Content Standards," *Education Week*, April 17, 2007.

10. Jaekyung Lee and Yin Wu, "Is the Common Core Racing America to the Top? Tracking Changes in State Standards, School Practices, and Student Achievement," *Education Policy Analysis Archives* 25, no. 35, https://epaa.asu.edu/ojs/article/view/2834.

11. National Center for Education Statistics, *Mapping 2005 State Proficiency Standards onto the NAEP Scales*, NCES 2007-482 (Washington, DC: US Department of Education, 2007).

12. Lee and Wu, "Common Core Racing."

13. Joshua Bleiberg, *Does the Common Core Have a Common Effect? An Exploration of Effects on Academically Vulnerable Students*, EdWorkingPaper 20-213 (March 2020). Retrieved from Annenberg Institute at Brown University: https://doi.org /10.26300/v0an-cz33.

14. Bleiberg, 19.

15. Tom Loveless, "A Progress Report on the Common Core," *The 2014 Brown Center Report on American Education* (Washington, DC: Brown Center on Education Policy at Brookings, 2014), 26–34.

16. Tom Loveless, "Measuring Effects of the Common Core," *The 2015 Brown Center Report on American Education* (Washington, DC: Brown Center on Education Policy at Brookings, 2015), 18–24.

17. Minnesota adopted the CCSS-ELA but not the standards in math. Hence, analyses of reading scores have four nonadopters and analyses of math scores have five.

18. Tom Loveless, "Reading and Math in the Common Core Era," *The 2016 Brown Center Report on American Education* (Washington, DC: Brown Center on Education Policy at Brookings, 2016), 6–15.

19. For example, Indiana, Oklahoma, and South Carolina rescinded Common Core in 2014. They were categorized as nonadopters in IMP13 analyses of the 2013 to 2015 NAEP score changes.

20. One would also expect any demographic changes that did occur to look random across the implementation groups of states, thereby diminishing the potential for bias in comparing groups.

21. Tom Loveless, "Why Standards Produce Weak Reform," in *Bush-Obama School Reform: Lessons Learned*, ed. Frederick M. Hess and Michael Q. McShane (Cambridge, MA: Harvard Education Press, 2018), 107–124.

22. Several different counts of PARCC and SBAC states exist. The P/SB19 coding relies on Catherine Gewertz, "What Tests Did Each State Require in 2016–17? An Interactive Breakdown of States' 2016–17 Testing Plans," *Education Week*, February 15, 2017, updated March 7, 2019, https://www.edweek.org/ew/section/multimedia /what-tests-did-each-state-require-2016-17.html.

23. Asian/Pacific Islander scores are unavailable for twenty-seven states because of small numbers.

24. Lauren Camera, "Across the Board, Scores Drop in Math and Reading for U.S. Students," *US News & World Report*, October 30, 2019, https://www.usnews.com/news /education-news/articles/2019-10-30/across-the-board-scores-drop-in-math-and -reading-for-us-students.

CHAPTER 7

1. This argument is made in favor of common standards and assessments across several states. See Thomas J. Kane, "Never Judge a Book by Its Cover—Use Student Achievement Instead," Brookings Institution, March 3, 2016, https://www.brookings.edu /research/never-judge-a-book-by-its-cover-use-student-achievement-instead/; and Joshua Bleiberg and Darrell M. West, "In Defense of the Common Core," Brook-

ings Institution, March 6, 2014, https://www.brookings.edu/research/in-defense
-of-the-common-core-standards/.

2. Kenneth K. Wong and Tom Loveless, "The Politics of Textbook Policy: Proposing a
Framework," in *Textbooks in American Society* (Albany: SUNY Press, 1991), 27–41;
Gail Collins, "How Texas Inflicts Bad Textbooks on Us," *New York Review of Books*,
June 21, 2012.

3. Claire Suddath, "Outsourcing the Textbook," *Time*, September 4, 2008.

4. Full disclosure: the author was a member of the advisory panel to the Mathematica
study. Roberto Agodini et al., *Achievement Effects of Four Early Elementary School
Math Curricula: Findings for First and Second Graders*, NCEE 2011-4001 (Washington, DC: National Center for Education Evaluation and Regional Assistance, 2010).

5. David Blazar et al., *Learning by the Book: Comparing Math Achievement Growth by
Textbook in Six Common Core States* (Cambridge, MA: Center for Education Policy
Research, Harvard University, 2019). Nevada was unable to provide state test data
due to technological glitches.

6. Matthew M. Chingos and Grover J. Whitehurst, *Choosing Blindly: Instructional
Materials, Teacher Effectiveness, and the Common Core* (Washington, DC: Brown
Center on Education Policy, 2012).

7. Cory Turner, "The Common Core Curriculum Void," NPR, June 3, 2014, https://www
.npr.org/sections/ed/2014/06/03/318228023/the-common-core-curriculum-void.

8. *The Textbook Navigator/Journal: Development and Background* (East Lansing, MI:
Center for the Study of Curriculum, Michigan State University, 2015), http://
education.msu.edu/csc/pdf/Navigator-Report.pdf.

9. Michael Alison Chandler, "Are Math Textbooks Ready for Common Core?," *Washington Post*, February 14, 2014, https://www.washingtonpost.com/local/education
/are-math-textbooks-ready-for-common-core/2014/02/24/b937a3a0-9d61-11e
3-9ba6-800d1192d08b_story.html.

10. Morgan S. Polikoff, "How Well Aligned Are Textbooks to the Common Core Standards in Mathematics?," *American Educational Research Journal* 52, no. 6 (December 2015): 1185–1211, 1201.

11. See https://achievethecore.org/category/774/mathematics-focus-by-grade-level.

12. Liana Loewus, "Review of Math Programs Comes Under Fire," *Education Week*,
March 17, 2015.

13. See the description of EdReports' rating scales at https://www.edreports.org/modal
/rating-scale.

14. Yujing Ni and Yong-Di Zhou, "Teaching and Learning Fraction and Rational Numbers: The Origins and Implications of Whole Number Bias," *Educational Psychologist* 40, no. 1 (2005): 27–52; Meral Aksu, "Student Performance in Dealing with
Fractions," *Journal of Educational Research* 90, no. 6 (1997): 375–380.

15. Agile Mind HS Publisher Response, available at https://www.edreports.org/reports
/detail/ahJzfmVkcmVwb3J0cy0yMDY2MThyKAsSCVB1Ymxpc2hlchggDDAsSBlN
lcmllcxhJDAsSBlJlcG9ydBjAAgw#publishers-response-pane.

16. Excerpts are from Report Center, Agile Mind HS; full-length version at https://
www.edreports.org/reports/detail/ahJzfmVkcmVwb3J0cy0yMDY2MThyKAsSCVB
1Ymxpc2hlchgDDAsSBlNlcmllcxhJDAsSBlJlcG9ydBjAAgw#the-report.

17. Brendan Lowe, "Textbook Adoption Was Once about 'Going to the Right Dinner'
with Publishers. Now EdReports Is Disrupting the $8 Billion Industry by Putting

Teachers in Charge," The 74, September 8, 2019, https://www.the74million.org
/article/textbook-adoption-was-once-about-going-to-the-right-dinner-with
-publishers-now-edreports-is-disrupting-the-8-billion-industry-by-putting
-teachers-in-charge/.

18. See Mark Keierleber, "6 Reasons Why Singapore Math Might Just Be the Better
Way," The 74, July 11, 2015, https://www.the74million.org/article/6-reasons-why
-singapore-math-might-just-be-the-better-way/. See also Kathleen Porter-Magee,
"Common Core Confusion: It's a Math, Math World," Thomas B. Fordham Institute, May 30, 2014, https://fordhaminstitute.org/national/commentary/common
-core-confusion-its-math-math-world.

19. *Comparing the Common Core State Standards and Singapore's Mathematics Syllabus*
(Washington, DC: Achieve, 2010), https://www.achieve.org/publications/comparing
-common-core-state-standards-and-singapore's-mathematics-syllabus.

20. Ministry of Education, Singapore, *Mathematics Syllabus: Primary One to Six* (Singapore: Curriculum Planning and Development Division, 2012).

21. "Singapore Math: Primary Mathematics Common Core Edition Grade 2," Ed-
Reports, https://edreports.org/reports/detail/ahJzfmVkcmVwb3J0cy0yMDY2MThy
KAsSCVB1Ymxpc2hlchgcDAsSBlNlcmllcxhxDAsSBlJlcG9ydBikBAw.

22. See page 56 in Marta Pellegrini et al., "Effective Programs in Elementary Mathematics: A Meta-Analysis," Best Evidence Encyclopedia, May 2020, www.best
evidence.org/word/elem_math_May_26_2020_full.pdf.

23. Robert Slavin, "The Gap," *Robert Slavin's Blog*, September 5, 2019, https://robert
slavinsblog.wordpress.com/2019/09/05/the-gap/.

24. Mike Mullin, "How the Lexile System Harms Students," *League of Extraordinary
Writers* (blog), October 21, 2012, http://leaguewriters.blogspot.com/2012/10/how
-lexile-system-harms-students.html.

25. E. D. Hirsch Jr., *Why Knowledge Matters* (Cambridge, MA: Harvard University
Press, 2016), 75.

26. David Griffith and Ann M. Duffett, *Reading and Writing Instruction in America's
Schools* (Washington, DC: Thomas B. Fordham Institute, 2018), 21.

27. Julia H. Kaufman et al., *Changes in What Teachers Know and Do in the Common
Core Era: American Teacher Panel Findings from 2015 to 2017*, report RR2658
(RAND Corporation, 2018).

28. Robert Rothman defends Common Core against some of the myths that circulated
regarding the use of fiction and nonfiction in Robert Rothman, "Fiction (and Nonfiction) about the Common Core State Standards," Alliance for Excellent Education, December 11, 2012, https://all4ed.org/fiction-and-nonfiction-about-the
-common-core-state-standards/.

29. Griffith and Duffett, *Reading and Writing*.

30. The Algebra for All movement is detailed in Tom Loveless, "The Misplaced Math
Student," *2008 Brown Center Report on American Education* (Washington, DC:
Brookings Institution, 2009), 20–31.

31. Charles T. Clotfelter, Helen F. Ladd, and Jacob L. Vigdor, "The Aftermath of Accelerating Algebra: Evidence from District Policy Initiatives," *Journal of Human Resources* 50, no. 1 (2015): 159–188; Ellaine Allensworth et al., "College Preparatory
Curriculum for All: Academic Consequences of Requiring Algebra and English I

for Ninth Graders in Chicago," *Educational Evaluation and Policy Analysis* 31, no. 4 (2009): 367–391.

32. *Common Core State Standards for Mathematics, Appendix A* (Washington, DC: Common Core State Standards Initiative, 2010), 3.

33. For a description of Bloom's taxonomy, see Patricia Armstrong, "Bloom's Taxonomy," Center for Teaching, Vanderbilt University, accessed October 1, 2020, https://cft.vanderbilt.edu/guides-sub-pages/blooms-taxonomy/.

34. "What Are the Surveys of Enacted Curriculum (SEC)?," Council of Chief State School Officers, accessed October 1, 2020, http://programs.ccsso.org/projects/surveys_of_enacted_curriculum/.

35. "About the Iowa Tests of Basic Skills (ITBS)," Bright Education, accessed October 1, 2020, https://brighted.funeducation.com/Practice/Iowa-Test-of-Basic-Skills-ITBS; see levels 7 and 8.

36. "What Does the NAEP Mathematics Assessment Measure?," National Center for Education Statistics, Accessed October 1, 2020, https://nces.ed.gov/nationsreportcard/mathematics/whatmeasure.aspx.

37. The Common Core State Standards Initiative standards-setting criteria are available at http://www.corestandards.org/assets/Criteria.pdf (accessed October 1, 2020).

38. See Samuel Otten, Zandra de Araujo, and Corey Webel, "Analyzing Claims about Cognitive Demand and Student Learning," in *Proceedings of the 39th Annual Meeting of the North American Chapter of the International Group for the Psychology of Mathematics Education*, ed. Enrique Galindo and Jill Newton (Indianapolis, IN: Hoosier Association of Mathematics Teacher Educators, 2017), 1391–1398.

39. Andrew C. Porter, "In Common Core, Little to Cheer About," *Education Week*, August 9, 2011, https://www.edweek.org/ew/articles/2011/08/10/37porter_ep.h30.html.

40. Porter, "Little to Cheer About"; italics in original.

41. Thomas J. Kane et al., *Teaching Higher: Educators' Perspectives on Common Core Implementation* (Cambridge, MA: Center for Education Policy Research, 2016).

42. Barbara Oakley, "How I Rewired My Brain to Become Fluent in Math," *Nautilus*, October 2, 2014, http://nautil.us/issue/17/big-bangs/how-i-rewired-my-brain-to-become-fluent-in-math.

43. Rose French, "Survey: Teachers Do Not Favor 'Integrated' Math in High Schools," *Atlanta Journal Constitution*, September 30, 2014, https://www.ajc.com/news/local-education/survey-teachers-not-favor-integrated-math-high-schools/uKWGGxSZ7uU22Kdtlvny0I/; Liana Heitin Loewus, "Georgia to Abandon Mandate on Teaching Integrated Math," *Education Week*, February 24, 2015, http://blogs.edweek.org/edweek/curriculum/2015/02/georgia_to_abandon_mandate_on.html.

44. "NAEP Data Explorer," Nation's Report Card, accessed October 1, 2020, https://www.nationsreportcard.gov/ndecore/xplore/nde.

CHAPTER 8

1. For a review of state accountability under ESSA, see Paul Manna and Arnold Shober, *Answering the Call? Explaining How States Have (or Have Not) Taken Up the ESSA Accountability Challenge*, background paper for the Hoover Education Success Initiative (Stanford, CA: Hoover Institution, 2020). See also Adam Kirk Edgerton, "The Essence of ESSA: More Control at the District Level?," *Phi Delta*

Kappan, September 23, 2019, https://kappanonline.org/the-essence-of-essa-more
-control-at-the-district-level/.

2. "2019 State of the Market Report," EdReports.org, May 26, 2020, https://www
.edreports.org/resources/article/2019-state-of-the-market-report. See also Morgan
Polikoff and Jennifer Dean, *The Supplemental Curriculum Bazaar: Is What's Online
Any Good?* (Washington, DC: Thomas B. Fordham Institute, 2019).

3. Hailey Sweetland Edwards, "Teachers Union Pulls Full-Throated Support for Common Core," *Time*, July 11, 2014, https://time.com/2976909/common-core-american
-federation-teachers/.

4. Katharine Beals and Barry Garelick, "Explaining Your Math: Unnecessary at Best,
Encumbering at Worst," *Atlantic*, November 11, 2015, https://www.theatlantic.com
/education/archive/2015/11/math-showing-work/414924/.

5. Mark Bertin, "When Will We Ever Learn: Dissecting the Common Core State Standards with Dr. Louisa Moats," *Psychology Today* (blog), January 21, 2014, https://
www.psychologytoday.com/us/blog/child-development-central/201401/when
-will-we-ever-learn.

6. Alex Baumhardt, "A Conversation with Emily Hanford on Reading Instruction in
the U.S.," APM Reports, October 24, 2019, https://www.apmreports.org/episode
/2019/10/23/hanfordandreading.

7. Sarah Schwartz, "The Most Popular Reading Programs Aren't Backed by Science,"
Education Week, December 3, 2019.

8. David K. Cohen, "Standards-Based School Reform: Policy, Practice, and Performance," in *Holding Schools Accountable: Performance-Based Reform in Education*,
ed. Helen F. Ladd (Washington, DC: Brookings Institution, 1996), 99–127.

9. Tom Loveless, "High Achievers, Tracking, and the Common Core," Brookings Institution, January 29, 2015, https://www.brookings.edu/research/high-achievers
-tracking-and-the-common-core/.

10. Sarah Schwartz, "Parent Who Criticized His Son's Math Program Is Sued by Company," *Education Week*, September 12, 2019, https://www.edweek.org/ew/articles
/2019/09/10/parent-who-criticized-his-sons-math-program.html.

11. Rajeev Darolia et al., "High School Course Access and Postsecondary STEM Enrollment and Attainment," *Educational Evaluation and Policy Analysis* 42, no. 1
(March 2020), 22–45.

12. Brian Jacob, et al., "Are Expectations Alone Enough? Estimating the Effect of a
Mandatory College-Prep Curriculum in Michigan," *Educational Evaluation and
Policy Analysis* 39, no. 2 (2017): 333–360.

13. Dr. Francis Collins, "Study Finds No Benefit from Dietary Supplements," *NIH Director's Blog*, April 16, 2019, https://directorsblog.nih.gov/2019/04/16/study-finds
-no-benefit-for-dietary-supplements/.

14. Michael Lipsky, *Street-Level Bureaucracy* (New York: Russell Sage Foundation, 1980).

15. *Common Challenges to Implementing College- and Career-Readiness Standards*
(Philadelphia: Center on Standards, Alignment, and Learning, 2019), https://eric
.ed.gov/?q=%22Center+on+Standards%2c+Alignment%2c+Instruction%2c+and
+Learning%22&id=ED598946.

16. Shawn McCoy, "From PARCC's Ashes, a New Model for Interstate Collaboration
Emerges," InsideSources, April 16, 2019, https://www.insidesources.com/from
-parccs-ashes-a-new-model-for-interstate-collaboration-emerges/.

17. *2017–18 Summative Technical Report* (Santa Cruz, CA: Smarter Balanced Assessment Consortium, 2018), https://www.smarterbalanced.org/wp-content/uploads/2019/08/2017-18-Summative-Assessment-Technical-Report.pdf.

18. Sherman Dorn, "Sherman Dorn: Why It's Counterproductive to Confuse Different Educational Challenges," NEPC, November 19, 2013, https://nepc.info/blog/why-counterproductive-confuse.

19. *The MetLife Survey of the American Teacher* (New York: MetLife Inc., 2013), 10.

20. Leland Cogan, William Schmidt, and Richard Houang, *Implementing the Common Core State Standards for Mathematics: What We Know about Teachers of Mathematics in 41 States*, working paper 33 (Michigan State University, January 2013); italics in original.

21. See chapter 2. See also David K. Cohen and Deborah Loewenberg Ball, "Policy and Practice: An Overview," *Educational Evaluation and Policy Analysis* 13, no. 3 (Fall 1990): 237.

22. James Q. Wilson, *Bureaucracy: What Government Agencies Do and Why They Do It* (New York: Basic Books, 1989), 222.

23. Wilson, 224.

24. David Tyack and Larry Cuban, *Tinkering Toward Utopia: A Century of Public School Reform* (Cambridge: Harvard University Press, 1995).

25. Lillian Mongeau, "Common Core Standards Bring Dramatic Changes to Elementary School Math," EdSource, January 20, 2014, https://edsource.org/2014/common-core-standards-bring-dramatic-changes-to-elementary-school-math-2/63665.

26. Richard Ingersoll et al., *Seven Trends: The Transformation of the Teaching Force—Updated October 2018* (Philadelphia: Consortium for Policy Research in Education, University of Pennsylvania, 2018).

27. Robert S. Siegler et al., "Early Predictors of High School Mathematics Achievement," *Psychological Science* 23, no. 7 (2012): 691–697.

28. Thomas B. Hoffer et al., *Final Report on the National Survey of Algebra Teachers for the National Math Panel* (Chicago: NORC at the University of Chicago, 2007), https://www2.ed.gov/about/bdscomm/list/mathpanel/final-report-algebra-teachers.pdf.

29. Sally Ho, "AP Analysis Shows How Bill Gates Influences Education Policy," Associated Press, May 16, 2018, https://apnews.com/a4042e82ffaa4a34b50ceac464761957/.

ACKNOWLEDGMENTS

I want to thank my longtime friend Rick Hess for more than two decades of discussion that has influenced my thinking on education policy and its implementation—and for encouraging me to write this book. I am indebted to Caroline Chauncey and Sumita Mukherji of Harvard Education Press for carefully guiding me through every stage of the production process, from submission to the final copy edits. Two anonymous reviewers offered helpful comments and suggestions that forced me to sharpen my thinking on several topics. Melinda Rankin's outstanding copyediting improved the manuscript in countless ways. Andrew Conkey provided sterling research and editorial assistance, and without his much-appreciated help, this book could not have happened.

ABOUT THE AUTHOR

Tom Loveless is an education researcher and former senior fellow at the Brookings Institution (1999–2014). From 2000 to 2017, he authored *The Brown Center Report on American Education*, an annual report analyzing important trends in education. Loveless has published widely in scholarly journals and appeared in popular media to discuss school reform, student achievement, and other education topics.

Loveless holds a PhD in education from the University of Chicago, an MA in special education from California State University, Sacramento, and an AB in English from the University of California, Berkeley. From 1979 to 1988, Loveless was a classroom teacher in the San Juan Unified School District, near his hometown of Sacramento, California. From 1992 to 1999, Loveless was an assistant and associate professor of public policy at Harvard University's John F. Kennedy School of Government. At Brookings, Loveless served as director of the Brown Center on Education Policy from 1999 to 2008.

From 2004 to 2012, Loveless represented the United States at the General Assembly of the International Association for the Evaluation of Educational Assessment, a sixty-nation organization that governs international testing. From 2006 to 2008, he was a member of the president's National Mathematics Advisory Panel.

You can follow Tom on Twitter at @tomloveless99.

INDEX